A FourFourTwo Book

Authors: Jim Drewett and Alex Leith
Publishing Editor: Rahiel Nazir
Design: Karen Bates

Superstars Of The Premier League

This edition first published by Parragon 1997
Parragon
Unit 13-17 Avonbridge Trading Estate
Atlantic Road
Avonmouth
Bristol BS11 9QD
Produced by ***FourFourTwo***, Haymarket Magazines Ltd
and Magpie Books.

Cover pictures and illustrations courtesy of Action Images and Tim Healy
Repro by F1 Colour

ISBN 075252 249 3

Contents

At the last minute Sheringham transfers to United. Replacing Eric Cantona is an unenviable task, but Teddy Sheringham should be equal to it. Vision, flair and great finishing are all qualities he posesses in abundance. Old Trafford expects...

Introduction to the

Welcome to the third editon of *FourFourTwo* magazine's 'Superstars of the Premier League', your essential guide to the hottest talent in the greatest football league in the world... and this one is the biggest and best yet.

For just as the Premiership has grown in style and stature over the last few seasons, so the 40 or so 'stars' featured in this annual offering have become more and more 'super'. Just take a look at the list of players featured in this edition. A few years ago, for instance, who'd have thought that a book on players in the Premiership would include some of the world's biggest names including Italian, Brazilian, Dutch and French international stars. And from Asprilla to Zola, from Jones to Le Tissier, you'll find them all in here.

You'll also find our predictions as to what these 'Superstars' will achieve this season. Will they inspire their teams to glorious success or watch helpless as the men around them conspire to send them tumbling towards life in the dreaded Nationwide League?

To arrive at our conclusions we were going to run Premiership statistics into an enormous mainframe computer, then have them analysed by a panel of football

PREMIER LEAGUE

Predicted final table 1996/97

1	Liverpool	11	Chelsea
2	Manchester Utd	12	West Ham
3	Newcastle Utd	13	Nott'm Forest
4	Blackburn R	14	Coventry
5	Aston Villa	15	Wimbledon
6	Tottenham	16	Sheffield Wed
7	Arsenal	17	Sunderland
8	Middlesbrough	18	Derby County
9	Everton	19	Southampton
10	Leeds Utd	20	Leicester City

How they actually finished

1	Manchester Utd	11	Leeds Utd
2	Newcastle Utd	12	Derby County
3	Arsenal	13	Blackburn R
4	Liverpool	14	West Ham
5	Aston Villa	15	Everton
6	Chelsea	16	Southampton
7	Sheffield Wed	17	Coventry
8	Wimbledon	18	Sunderland
9	Leicester City	19	Middlesbrough
10	Tottenham	20	Nott'm Forest

experts and finally cross-reference them against league tables covering the last 100 years of football. Then we decided 'what the heck' we'd just do what we did last year - stick the kettle on, sit down with a packet of 'jammy dodgers' and work it out ourselves.

OK, so perhaps it wasn't the most scientific method around, but thankfully football isn't a science and our light-hearted gaze into the crystal ball wasn't actually that far out last year.

OK, so we predicted that Liverpool would come top. But how could we have known that, with the title up for grabs, David James would be kidnapped by vampires and hence develop a terrible fear of crosses for the last month of the season? OK, so we said that Leicester, Derby and Southampton would go down and they all stayed up (but only just.) We were wrong about Blackburn finishing 4th and Sheffield Wednesday struggling down in 16th place. We were, however, right to predict that, er, Aston Villa would end up 5th and that the likes of Coventry, West Ham and Wimbledon would escape the drop. It goes to show that, just like all so-called football experts, we sometimes get it wrong. We are, after all, only human, just like the 'Superstars' in this book... it's just that they are better at football than we are at making predictions!

Vital Statistics

Age 30

Date of Birth 10.10.66

Place of Birth London

Nickname Rodders [as in the *Only Fools and Horses* character]

League Games & Goals
Arsenal 394 [27]

Tony Adams' 1996/97 season
Plagued by an ankle injury but when fit showed he's developed into a classy, as well as a committed, defender

Honours
Division One Champions 1988/89 & 1990/91
FA Cup 1993
Football League Cup 1987 & 1993
European Cup Winners' Cup 1994

Transfers
Signed as an apprentice for Arsenal, received his first pro contract on 30.1.84

Position/Role
Dying for the cause every Saturday, arm raised until the last

Word most often used to describe him
Rock

Word never used to describe him
Softy

> "He's a great captain, a born leader."
>
> *Frank McLintock*

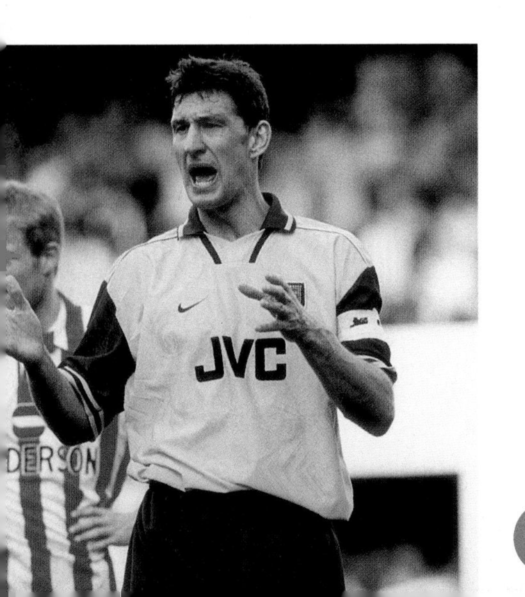

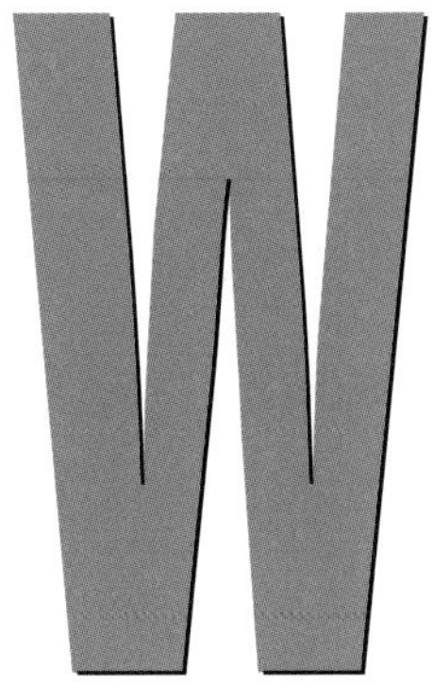

hen Arsene Wenger arrived at Highbury at the start of last season, many people believed that the time for rebuilding at Arsenal had arrived. The Frenchman may indeed be on the verge of donning his hard hat and beginning demolition work on an ageing team, but he'll do it safe in the knowledge that the foundations for Arsenal's future are already in place - in the shape of Tony Adams.

For while the papers are cluttered with names of defenders allegedly set for the axe, the one name never mentioned is that of the Gooners' inspirational centre back. Try to imagine Tony Adams in a Manchester United shirt or a Liverpool one and you just can't do it, your mind draws a blank, because Tony Adams is Arsenal right down to those size 12 socks and an Arsenal team without its long-standing skipper is, frankly, inconceivable.

Former Gunners' captain Frank McLintock agrees: "He's Mr Irreplaceable, it's as simple as that. If he ever wanted to leave Arsenal, and I can't believe in his heart of heart that he ever would, the board should break the bank to keep him. He is a great captain, a born leader."

Adams' leadership qualities have never been in doubt (he towered as England's centre back in Euro '96), but thanks to the *Daily Mirror's* graphics department and a few dodgy performances on live TV many years ago, the 'donkey' tag has taken a long time to lose.

"Those things that were said about him, the donkey ears and all that, they just served as a stimulant to him," says Don Howe who was assistant manager at Arsenal in 1984, when Adams made his debut aged just 17. Howe describes him as "a truly great defender. He took it all on the chin and got on with it."

Adams is a product of an Arsenal youth team which included the likes of Paul Merson, Paul Davis, Michael Thomas and David Rocastle, and Howe recalls: "It was a real top notch bunch but Tony was the leader even then." Except for Merson all of them have now fled the Arsenal nest, but Arsenal can't bring themselves to imagine that Adams could ever be led astray.

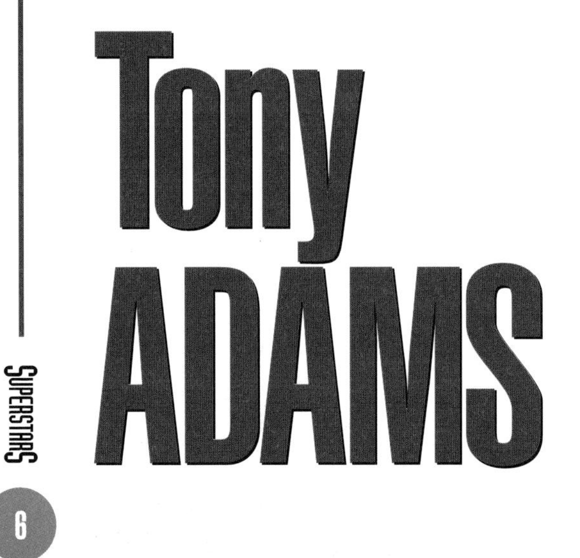

JVC
6

Vital Statistics

Age 25

Date of Birth 3.3.72

Place of Birth
Southampton

Nickname
Shaggy [after the Scooby Doo character]

League Games & Goals
Portsmouth 62 [6]
Tottenham Hotspur 129 [22]

Darren Anderton's 1996/97 season
Just like the one before he had a nightmare with injuries, managing just thirteen league appearances and a measly three goals. A return to full fitness is what he [and all Spurs and England fans] pray for

Transfers
Portsmouth to Tottenham [£1.75m]

Position/Role
Either darting towards the opposition goal... or the treatment room

Word most often used to describe him
Sickly

Word never used to describe him
Fat

At first glance, Darren Anderton looks like a playground bully's dream. Skinny, pale and kind of gangly, he's the kind of player who'd get picked last in a game of park football and you'd expect him to burst into tears every time one of the big boys tried to tackle him.
Any such thinking by a defender can be filed directly in the wishful section. With a quick shuffle and a turn of pace that puts his Scooby Doo namesake to shame, Anderton can whip past his man and down to the by-line before you can say "don't judge a book by its cover." Even after yet another injury-dominated season, which has made the sight of Anderton in the Tottenham line-up about as rare as a Ronnie Rosenthal goal at White Hart Lane, he's still high on the list of the finest attackers in the country. If Anderton can shake off the groin problems which, amongst other injuries, have recently brought a sudden and dramatic halt to a blossoming career, he still has the talent to put him right at the top of the English game. And how Spurs need him, as the club's captain freely acknowledges.

"He's very deceptive," says Gary Mabbutt. "In a way he's like Chris Waddle, in that he looks ungainly yet he's extremely quick. He loves taking people on and beating them and he's one of the best crossers of the ball I've seen in my career. He's also got a lethal shot."

Anderton is the antithesis of the traditional five-foot-nothing-sixpence-ha'penny winger, but is hardly built in the manner of a playmaking midfielder either, though he has excelled for Spurs in a central role, drawing comparisons with the old master, Sir Glenn, at White Hart Lane.

And with the maestro himself now in charge of the England squad – a squad in which he was an ever-present influence before, if you'll excuse the expression, his groin started niggling – Anderton will be determined to force his way back onto the international scene this season. "It's a totally different game," he says. "You're playing against better players, sure, but you're playing with better players too. I've enjoyed playing with Gazza, Paul Ince, David Platt. They've really brought out the best in me."

Maybe, but Spurs and England fans will be hoping there's much more still to come.

"He loves taking people on and beating them... He's also got a lethal shot."

Gary Mabbutt

Vital Statistics

Age 18

Date of Birth 14.3.79

Place of Birth Paris

League Games & Goals
Paris St Germain [France] 10 [1]

International record
Anelka has scored nine times in 18 appearances for the French youth team and his one appearance for the U20s side netted him two goals

Anelka's 1996/97 season
Having been pulled out of the PSG team in disgrace as news of his proposed transfer to Arsenal emerged, Anelka made the move to London and settled in slowly... eventually making his debut away at Chelsea towards the end of the season

Position/role
Making Ian Wright look and feel very, very old

Word most often used to describe him
Lively

Word never used to describe him
Loyal

> "I believe he will be a truly great player for Arsenal."
>
> *Arsene Wenger*

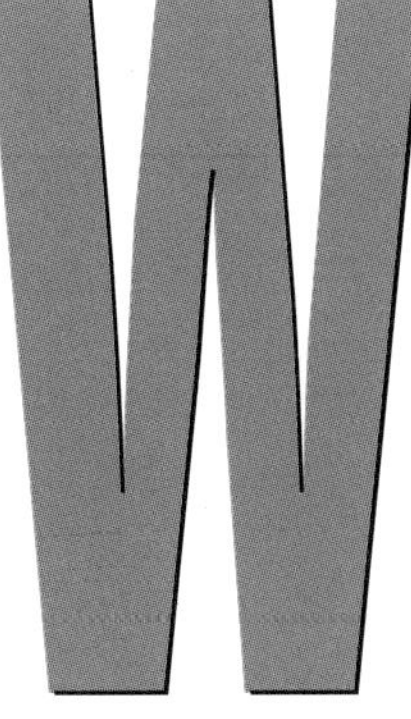
When it was revealed that Arsene Wenger was about to lure 18-year-old wonder boy striker Nicolas Anelka from Paris St Germain, there was uproar in France. Anelka is so highly rated across the Channel, and so great was the loss felt by PSG and French football as a whole, that his move has sparked a complete overhaul of the transfer system. Anelka had come through the ranks at PSG and under French legislation was obliged to sign professional for them at the end of last season. He could not go to any other French club, but when Arsenal got involved they were powerless to stop him from moving to England and had to accept a paltry £1.5 million rather than see him go on a free transfer at the end of the season.

"It will not happen again," says French Technical Director, Gerald Houllier who is in charge of rewriting the rules to make sure young French players stay in France at least in the early stages of their careers.

So what is it about Anelka that almost caused an international incident between England and France. Well, the 6ft 1in youngster is quite simply the hottest young striker in Europe. After just ten appearances in the PSG first team and one goal (against Lens), he had the coaches of the biggest teams in Europe drooling. Not that they didn't know about him already. Anelka had already proved a sensation at international level, scoring nine times in 18 games for the French youth team and when he made his debut for the Under 20s against Denmark in December 1996, he got off to a flyer by scoring twice.

Since moving to Arsenal, Anelka has been broken in gently. A regular in the reserves for the latter half of last season, he made his debut appearance as a substitute against Chelsea and ended up making three appearances from the bench by the end of the season.

And even in the space of those three brief appearances, the young Frenchman (a striker of electric pace and dazzling skill), showed to the Highbury faithful that there will be life after Wright when Arsenal's legendary number 8 finally has to hang up his boots.

JVC

Vital Statistics

Age 27

Date of Birth 10.11.69

Place of Birth Tulua [Colombia]

Nickname Black Gazelle

League Games & Goals
Nacional De Medellin [Colombia]
Parma [Italy] 84 [25]
Newcastle 36 [7]

International record
Asprilla has played for Colombia more than 40 times, scoring on 15 occasions

Honours
Colombian championship with Nacional, UEFA, European Cup Winners' and Super Cups with Parma

Position/Role
Going all rubbery-legged to bamboozle defenders [as well as his own team-mates]

Word most often used to describe him
Rubbery

Word never used to describe him
Predictable

"You may have to wait 50 years for another Asprilla to come along."

Gilbert Roman (Tino's former coach)

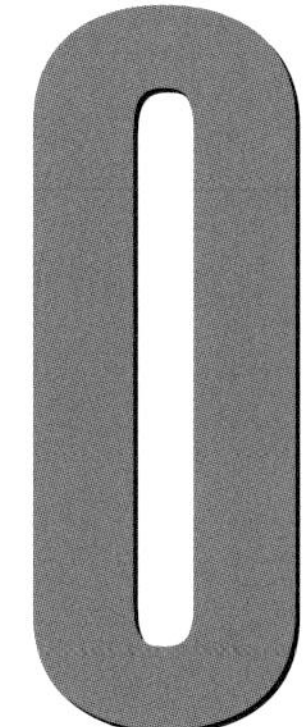

One spell of five minutes in a UEFA Cup game against Metz last season epitomised the topsy-turvy nature of Faustino Asprilla's football career.

Newcastle had gained a 1-1 draw in France but were living dangerously against the quickfire Frenchmen. On 80 minutes, the Colombian reacted quicker than everyone around him to nod a Peacock shot into the net. As the crowd roared their approval he ripped off his shirt, ran to the corner flag, put the shirt on top of it, uprooted it and started waving it like a flag. It was the most exuberant goal celebration St. James' Park had ever seen, and Asprilla was booked for his trouble, and out of the next game.

Two minutes later he was celebrating again - though this time the goal was more exuberant than its aftermath. He burst through the middle of the Metz defence, drew the goalkeeper, then planted the ball past him into the goal. The French were beaten and the crowd were looking forward to the possibility of the Colombian's first hat-trick for the club.

Alas, a couple of minutes after scoring the second, Asprilla pulled a hamstring and was stretchered off with the sound of 36,000 fans chanting 'Teeeeee-no' accompanying him off the field. The Geordie crowd absolutely adore the Colombian international, and so would you if he was in your team. Asprilla, with his strange rubbery legs, has the uncanny knack of making easy things seem difficult and difficult things seem easy. He doesn't so much run through defences as trip-up through defences; the ball seemingly tied to his foot on an elastic band rather than a piece of string; he plays football like a professional juggler pretending to be on the point of dropping everything but making sure he never does.

If he scored goals as regularly against Premiership defences as easily as he does against foreign ones – Asprilla scored five goals in the UEFA Cup and eight in the World Cup for Colombia last season – then he'd be worth three times the £7.5 million Keegan paid for him in January 1996. Maybe it's that and the challenge of having to get past the extra man in defence that spurs on the extravagant South American.

Faustino ASPRILLA

adidas
NEWCASTLE BROWN ALE

UMBRO
DANKA
UMBRO

Vital Statistics

Age 23

Date of Birth 11.2.74

Place of Birth Hull

League Games & Goals
Tottenham 87 [20]
Middlesbrough 32 [7]
Everton 35 [5]

Best known for
Being the 'new Peter Beardsley' and looking exactly like Craig Hignett when he played for 'Boro

Nicky Barmby's 1996/97 season
A memorable move to Everton, an unbelievable start for the Blues and then a run of form he'll want to forget. Did score for England against Moldava though, in Glenn Hoddle's first game in charge but later lost his place in the squad

Transfers
Tottenham to Middlesbrough [£4m]
Middlesbrough to Everton [£4.5m]

Position/Role
Peter Beardsley but with all his teeth still in place

Word[s] most often used to describe him
New Beardo

Word[s] never used to describe him
Past it

There was something not quite right about the Everton team sheet towards the end of last season. For sitting on the bench for a side which had floundered from one disaster to another was none other then Nick Barmby, England star and one of the game's brightest young talents.

Whatever the reasons for Barmby's disappointing start to his career on Merseyside, after his move from Middlesbrough last season, great things are still expected of the livewire striker. And it's certainly not like Barmby to be catching the eye because of anything other than his sublime talent.

Former England boss Terry Venables, who gave the Hull-born 23-year-old both his Spurs and England debuts, recalls the first time he saw him playing in the youth team at Tottenham's training ground. "He was the sort of player who stops you in his tracks," he recalls. "I knew straight away he had the potential to be a real talent. Arsenal wanted him, United were also very keen and Alex Ferguson is still bitter about him getting away. He was a natural, one of those players who only comes around once every few years."

After four years at Spurs, including one as part of Ossie Ardiles' 'famous five' strikeforce including Jürgen Klinsmann, homesick Barmby returned north to become Bryan Robson's first big name, big money signing at Middlesbrough. He started with a bang at 'Boro and made it into the England set-up, forcing the man he is most likened to – Peter Beardsley – out of Venables' Euro '96 squad. Then, early the following season, Robson, perhaps feeling he couldn't fit Barmby into the same side as Juninho, sold him to Everton.

Glenn Hoddle kept him in the England team and Teddy Sheringham has nothing but praise for his former Spurs colleague. "He's got unbelievable awareness of what's going on around him," says Sheringham. "He's got great control, is a good header of the ball and is a very neat finisher."

With Everton in the process of rebuilding, you get the feeling that if and when they do have a revival in fortunes, Nicky Barmby's going to have plenty to do with it.

"He's got great control, is a good header of the ball and is a very neat finisher."

Teddy Sheringham

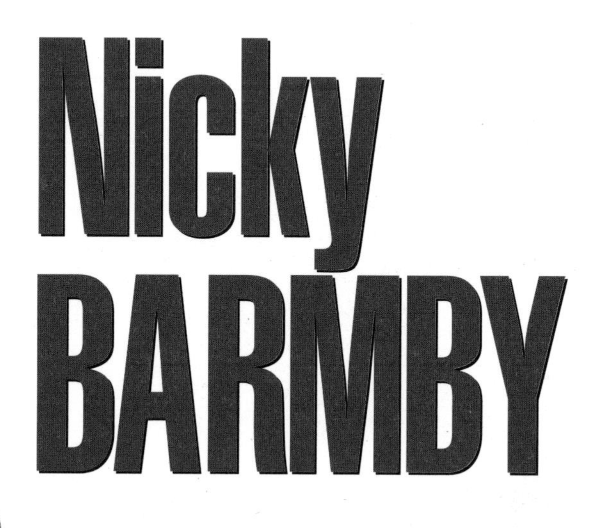

Vital Statistics

Age 33

Date of Birth 7.9.63

Place of Birth Jamaica

Nickname Barnsey

League Games & Goals
Watford 233 [65]
Liverpool 313 [84]

International record
Despite playing more than 50 times for England, Barnes never quite reproduced his club form for his country despite scoring one of England's greatest ever goals against Brazil in 1984

Honours
English championship [1988, 1990]
FA Cup [1989, 1992]
League Cup [1995]

Transfers
Watford to Liverpool [£900,000]

Position/Role
Neatly keeping the Liverpool's neat-passing midfield ticking over... but for how much longer?

Word most often used to describe him
Cool

Word never used to describe him
Sprightly

The worst thing that John Barnes ever did was to run through the Brazilian defence in the Maracana stadium in Rio, and score one of the most spectacular goals ever seen in the country of spectacular goals. Once he'd done that everybody expected him to do it again and when he didn't, almost every international performance he made was judged a disappointment. And over a ten year period the Jamaican-born player made 79 appearances for his adopted country.

It's ten years, too, that Barnes has been pulling on the red shirt of Liverpool. But the weight of expectation is never as high at club level, even at Anfield, and Barnes has rarely been short of brilliant for Liverpool in the 300-odd matches he has played for the team, first as a fast-moving forward, then as a slow-moving defensive midfielder.

Barnes now skippers the Reds from a position in front of the back four and it's his job to get the ball and give it to a younger pair of legs. Where some teams rely on a hard-man to do that job (and some Liverpool fans maintain that the club would be more successful if they had a Graeme Souness figure in Barnes' position), Liverpool realise that their skipper has the ability to make space for himself and deliver accurate passes nine times out of ten, which counteracts the need for more brawn and less brain at the back of midfield. Or as Barnes himself puts it, "if we had a ball-winner we might lose that Liverpool fluency. Liverpool's goal isn't to win the ball back - Liverpool's goal is not to give it away in the first place."

At 33, Barnes can't have many years left in him as a player – however pedestrian his role is at the club. But judging from the respect he commands from his team-mates and his obvious intelligence and articulation, the born-again midfielder would make a fine manager. Roy Evans beware.

> "I would love the chance to manage Liverpool."
>
> *John Barnes*

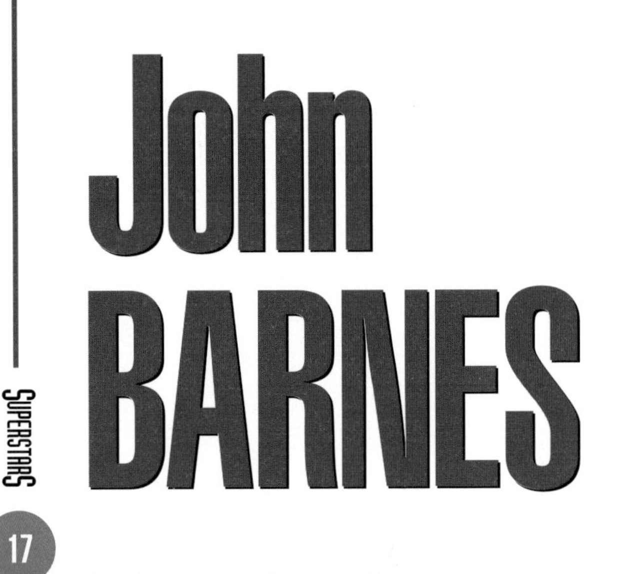

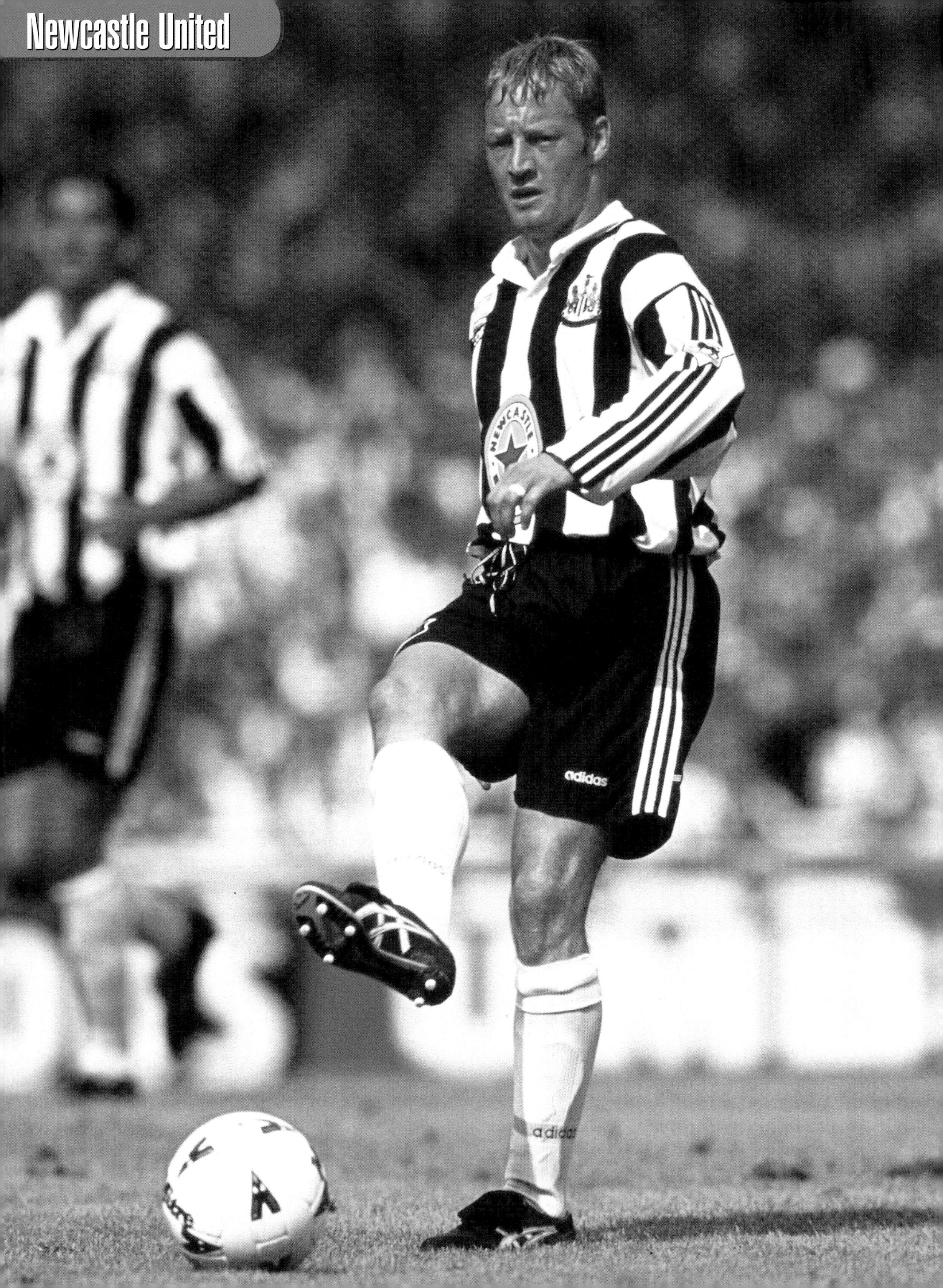
NEWCASTLE
adidas
adidas

Vital Statistics

Age 28

Date of Birth 2.12.68

Place of Birth Leeds

League Games & Goals
- Leeds 211 [4]
- Blackburn 54 [1]
- Newcastle 42 [2]

Best known for
Terrier-like tackling and neat passing... usually a few yards square of him to his closest team-mate

David Batty's 1996/97 season
Stunned himself, his team-mates and the entire football world by scoring a spectacular chip against Wimbledon. After that went back to doing what he does best, for Newcastle and Glenn Hoddle's England

Transfers
- Leeds to Blackburn [£2.75m]
- Blackburn to Newcastle [£3.75m]

Word most often used to describe him
Battling

Word never used to describe him
Stylish

People used to attack ex-England manager Graham Taylor for picking players such as Geoff Thomas, Carlton Palmer... and David Batty. The fact that Terry Venables experimented with the Yorkshire terrier (and that Batty is now one of the first names in Glenn Hoddle's squads), suggests Taylor's judgement might not have been quite as clouded as many imagine.

Mind you, in Taylor's day Batty was a rather different proposition. "At Leeds people saw me as just a ball-winner and that was probably a fair view," he says of his nine years at Elland Road which gained him both Second and First Division Championship medals. "The style of play was direct and I was there to win the ball and distribute it." The local lad earned himself a big reputation as the sort of guy who used bravery, aggression, and sheer born-and-bred Yorkshire grit. He made every fifty-fifty challenge sixty-forty in his favour and then gave the ball to his nearest team-mate.

In 1993, when Blackburn Rovers manager Kenny Dalglish came in for Batty and succeeded in buying him for £2.75 million, more than a few punters were surprised. But Batty soon learned to adapt to the Scotsman's gameplan. "Blackburn like to play the game on the ground a lot more and that's allowed me to develop my passing game," he said at the time.

He helped Rovers to the Championship but, after suffering for much of the season from a foot injury, he didn't feel he'd played enough games and refused to pick up a medal when the team lined-up to collect the trophy at Anfield.

And Batty's detractors were further surprised when the king of attacking football, Kevin Keegan, paid £3.75 million for the midfielder in a vain attempt to plug up the defensive gaps in his pursuit of the 1995/96 title. Batty won the Toon Army fans' hearts, but alas it wasn't to be third time lucky in the Championship stakes for the Yorkshireman. But who's to say that Batty won't help a second Kenny Dalglish side to win the title? And this time, he may even be immodest enough to pick up a medal for it.

> "At Leeds people saw me as just a ball-winner... I'm more than that now."
>
> *David Batty*

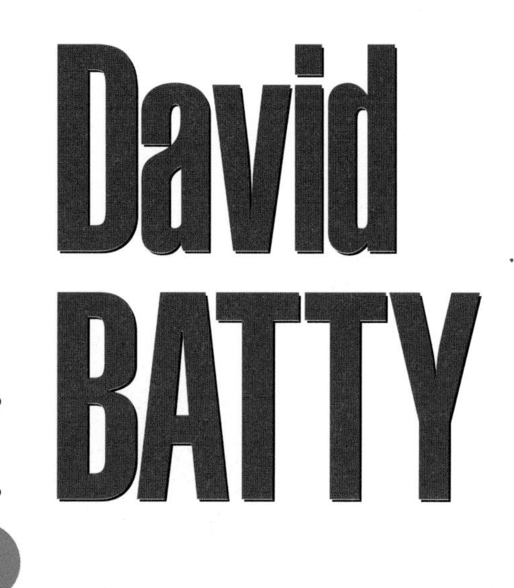

Vital Statistics

Age 22

Date of Birth 2.5.75

Place of Birth Leytonstone

Nickname Becks

League games & goals
Preston North End [loan] 5 [2]
Manchester United 71 [17]

International record
Since making his England debut in Glenn Hoddle's first match in charge, Beckham has pretty much been ever present, making 5 appearances

Transfers
Taken on as an apprentice at Manchester United, signed as a professional on 29.1.93

Honours
Premiership title [1996, 1997]
FA Cup [1996]

Position/Role
Swashbuckling his way though opposition defences from the right side of midfield and scoring goals that defy both gravity and logic... all to impress Posh Spice in the stand

Word most often used to describe him
Brilliant

Word never used to describe him
Over-rated

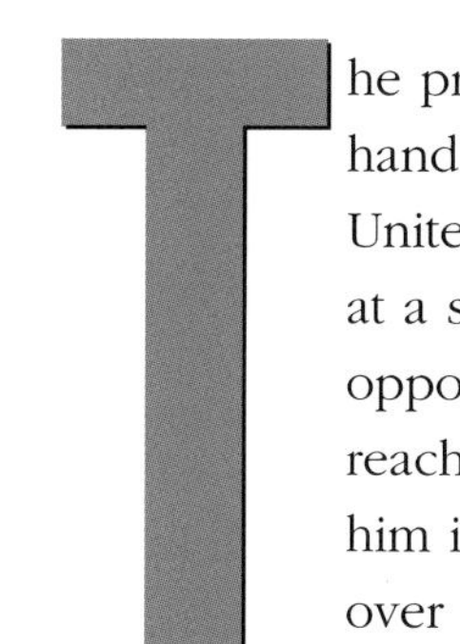

he promising young midfielder gets the ball on the right-hand side of his own half towards the end of Manchester United's opening game of the season against Wimbledon, at a sunny Selhurst Park. He looks up towards the opposing goal, looks down again and, before the ball reaches the halfway line, kicks it. What happens next turns him into a household name. The ball flies high into the air, over the United attackers and Wimbledon defenders, over the head of startled (and stranded) Dons' goalkeeper, Neil Sullivan and, most importantly, over the goal-line just under the bar. The wonderkid has scored a wondergoal, and it's the first of many he's to bag in the season. In years to come, maybe they'll use his surname as a verb to describe a brilliantly flighted shot. "And Smith has Beckhamed the ball into the net from 35 yards."

That moment marked the start of a remarkable season for the 22-year-old which saw him become one of the first names, not just on Alex Ferguson's team-sheet, but on Glenn Hoddle's too. What's more, he became a reluctant heart-throb: chased by the paparazzi and even rumoured by the tabloids to be having a fling with Posh Spice.

Beckham was born in the East End of London, but his dad, Ted, was a Cockney Red and young David wanted nothing more than to play at Old Trafford. So after training for three years with Tottenham, he was delighted to get the chance to train in the summer in Manchester after winning a Bobby Charlton soccer skills tournament. He's hardly looked back since – signing a five-year deal with United and a contract with Adidas which will make him a millionaire before he reaches his mid-twenties.

"I still work a lot on my game," he says. "After most sessions at United I stay behind." He spends plenty of that extra time practicing his long range shooting, as we saw at Selhurst Park (and all round the country) last season.

"His goal against Wimbledon was the best I've seen in my life," said Matt Le Tissier after unexpectedly winning Sky Sports Goal of 1996 Award in front of Beckham. "It will never be bettered. I don't know how I got the award. It's a bit embarrassing."

> "His goal against Wimbledon was the best I've seen in my life. It will never be bettered."
>
> *Matt Le Tissier*

Vital Statistics

Age 28

Date of Birth 19.5.69

Place of Birth Amsterdam

Nickname The ice man

League Games & Goals
Ajax [Holland] 185 [85]
Inter Milan [Italy] 52 [11]
Arsenal 61 [23]

Honours
European Cup Winners' Cup [Ajax] [1987]
UEFA Cup [Inter Milan] [1993]

Transfers
Ajax to Inter Milan [£8m]
Inter Milan to Arsenal [£7.5m]

Position/Role
On another planet, several light years from the one Ray Parlour and Nigel Winterburn inhabit

Word most often used to describe him
Chilled

Word never used to describe him
Over-excited

> "No matter what I do, I always know I can do better."
>
> *Dennis Bergkamp*

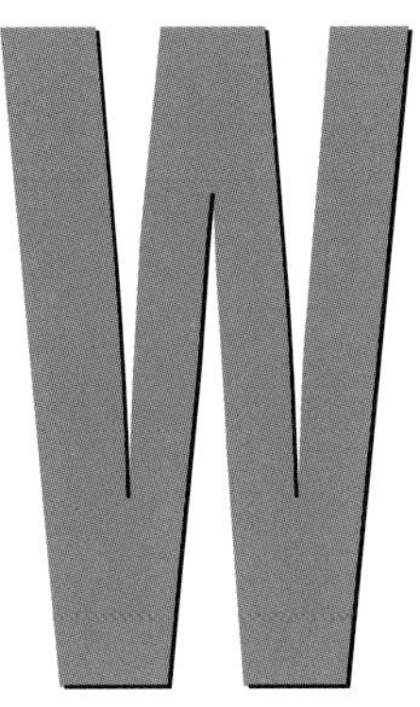

When Dennis Bergkamp arrived at Arsenal for a cool £7.5 million two seasons ago he had plenty to prove. After a miserable spell at Inter Milan, where he scored just 11 league goals in two seasons, there were plenty ready to gloat over the Gunners' wasted millions. But after a slow start, Bergkamp soon let his feet do the talking.

A creator, as well as a scorer of great goals, Bergkamp oozes class from every pore, a pure thoroughbred in a league which some would say is blessed with its fair share of donkeys. With 12 goals to his name last season, Bergkamp can sit back and be more than satisfied with his second season at Highbury. But will he?

"I always strive for perfection in the game," he says. "No matter what I do, I always know I can do better. That's what keeps me going. But if things don't come off there's no point getting annoyed or frustrated. I just bide my time because I know the chance will come again and then I will take it."

The chance to come to England (and pick up £30,000 a week in the process) was one the Dutch number ten jumped at. After two miserable years floundering in Series A with Inter Milan, he played out of position as an out-and-out striker instead of in his favoured deeper role. At one point, things were so bad at Milan that his team-mates renamed their 'donkey-of-the-week' award (for the worst player in the previous Sunday's game), to the 'Bergkamp-of-the-Week' award!

So when Arsenal came in for the striker who made his debut for Ajax aged 16 and scored 85 goals in 185 league games for the Dutch giants, he had no hesitation – even though he supported Tottenham as a kid and used to kick a ball around in a Glenn Hoddle shirt. He wanted to play in England and Arsenal were the first team to ask him, says Bergkamp.

In fact, he wanted to sign so much that he even got on a plane to London. Not unusual, you might think, except that he has a phobia about flying that is so bad that he refuses to play games in Holland he can't get to by boat or train. Maybe that's why he has said he wants to finish his career at Arsenal – he's too scared to leave London!

JVC

Nathan BLAKE

Vital Statistics

Age 25

Date of Birth 27.1.72

Place of Birth Cardiff

League games & goals
Cardiff City 131 [35]
Sheffield Utd 69 [34]
Bolton 60 [20]

Transfers
Chelsea to Cardiff City [free]
Cardiff City to Sheff Utd [£300,000]
Sheff Utd to Bolton [£1.3m]

Position/Role
Bursting through on goal and unleashing a ferocious shot into the top corner... all with the back of his shirt hanging out

Word most often used to describe him
Powerhouse

Word never used to describe him
Lethargic

> "His big backside gives him the strength to shrug off opponents"
>
> *FourFourTwo*

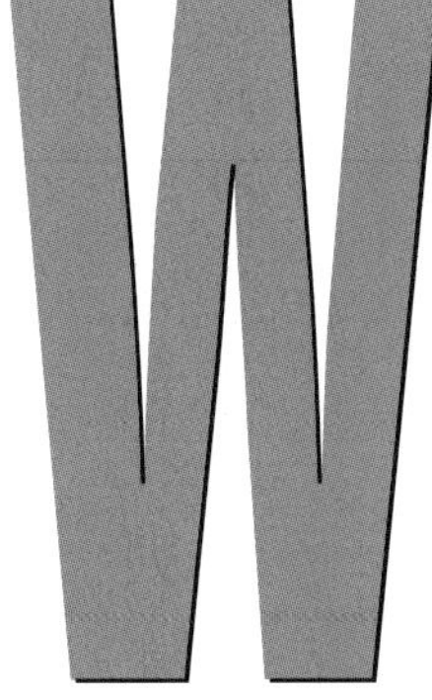
hen Nathan Blake had a bust up with Bobby Gould, after alleged racist remarks made by the Wales manager, Gould wasn't the only person hoping the 25-year-old striker wouldn't keep his promise not to play for the national side while the Englishman was in charge. With Rush and Hughes fast approaching pension age, Blake is easily the man most likely to score for the Dragons.

Blake was the scourge of Nationwide defences last season, scoring 20 goals in Bolton's successful push for promotion back into the big time, first time round. He's a big, strong attacker in the Shearer mould. He's good in the air but also skillful on the ground with a big backside capable of holding off challengers while help (usually in the form of John McGinlay) arrives. And promotion last summer was a boost for a player who's been more used to relegation.

In fact, Blake can be seen as being a bit of a jinx – the two Premier League sides he's signed for mid-season have ended up being relegated in the spring. He was a member of that Sheffield United side which went down on the last day of the season in 1994, and joined Bolton last Christmas only to return to his more accustomed Nationwide stamping ground the following term.

Blake's goals, of course, were crucial to Bolton's success in bouncing straight back up last season – but the Cardiff-born international started life as a bit of a utility man. Whilst at Cardiff (where he spent the first five years of his career), he was a full-back, a central midfielder and a winger before he tried his hand out at centre-forward. 17 goals in succession were enough to prove that he had what it takes, so much so that Dave Bassett brought him up two divisions to the Premier League.

And the Premier League is where he'll be playing next year – and for many years to come, if he can break his jinx and score enough goals to ensure Wanderers' safety.

Reebok

PUMA
LEEDS UNITED
AFC
Packard Bell

Vital Statistics

Age 20

Date of Birth 3.1.77

Place of Birth London

League Games & Goals
Charlton 46 [8]
Leeds 31 [4]

Transfers
Charlton to Leeds [£2.6m]

International record
Has played more than 10 times for the England U21 team and was called into Glenn Hoddle's squad for the first time last season

Bowyer's 1996/97 season
Took a while to settle at Leeds - a court appearance for a burger bar fracas didn't help - but was soon showing the form that made him Britain's most expensive teenager

Position/role
Tough little midfield dynamo, combining Batty-like strength and aggression with skill and vision

Word most often used to describe him
Young

Word never used to describe him
Mature

hen Howard Wilkinson smashed the teenage transfer record by signing 19-year-old Lee Bowyer from Charlton Athletic for £2.6 million in the summer of 1996, Leeds fans could have been forgiven for thinking their manager had gone off his rocker. But after seeing the action-man in the flesh last season, nobody's complaining any more – least of all George Graham, who inherited one of the most promising midfielders in the country.

Bowyer is no stranger to getting things done early. A product of the Lilleshall School of Excellence he signed as a full professional for the Addicks a year before time, played for the England U18 team at 16 and made the U21 team at 18.

But, shortly after making his debut for Charlton, Bowyer's career was threatened when he came up positive in a random drug test, a scandal which brought him his first (unwanted) national newspaper headlines.

Bowyer had the guts to roll up his sleeves, take his punishment and get on with his game. At the beginning of the 1995/96 season he played his way into the Charlton first team, one of a group of 'Curbishley's Colts', making almost as much a name for themselves as a certain group of youngsters up in Manchester. It soon became clear to the Valley faithful that they were witnessing the flowering of something really special - Bowyer showed great vision with his passing and started running Athletic from the middle.

Charlton's promotion hopes faded towards the end of the season but Bowyer got his chance to play in the Premiership when Wilkinson made his big close-season gamble. It was a gamble which paid off, as the youngster fitted neatly into the Yorkshire team's game-plan, eventually starting to run the show just as he had in London. His solid performances were rewarded in April with a Glenn Hoddle call-up to the senior squad (albeit the weakened one which met to play Mexico), and it shouldn't be too long before we see Bowyer pulling on the three-lioned shirt on a regular basis.

> "Lee has been sensational for us this season."
>
> *Leeds manager George Graham*

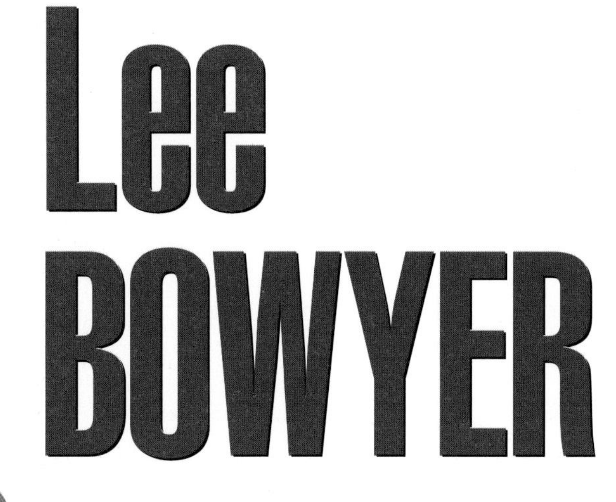

Carlsberg

Stan COLLYMORE

Vital Statistics

Age 26

Date of Birth 22.1.71

Place of Birth Stone

Nickname Stan the Man

League Games & Goals
Crystal Palace 20 [1]
Southend 30 [15]
Nottingham Forest 64 [40]
Liverpool 61 [26]

Transfers
Wolves to Stafford Rangers [free]
Stafford to Palace [£100,000]
Palace to Southend [£100,000]
Southend to Nott'm Forest [£2m]
Nott'm Forest to Liverpool [£8.5m]
Liverpool to Villa [£7m]

Position/Role
A lethal striking cog in any team... if he's in the mood

Word most often used to describe him
Unsettled

Word never used to describe him
Uncontroversial

There's something about November that seemed to send new Aston Villa star Stan Collymore off the rails at Liverpool. The plot usually went something like this – he'd make a blistering start to the season in the August sun. Then as autumn drew its curtains, he'd lose form and get dropped to the reserves. Come November he'd have a huge row with the club and it would look like the end of his Liverpool career. But then he'd win his place back in the team and finish the season strongly.

In November 1995, an interview in *FourFourTwo* magazine sparked the now infamous row. Collymore said that he was bewildered as to why Roy Evans had bothered to buy him in the first place if he wasn't going to play him. Evans had splashed out £8.5 million in the close season for the former Forest striker. Eventually they kissed and made up and he won his place back in the team.

In November 1996, Collymore found himself in the reserves again after Czech import Patrik Berger had played his way into the second striker position. Or at least he should have. The ex-Nottingham Forest hit-man didn't turn up for the match against Tranmere and his name had to be scratched off the team-sheet handed to the referee. Collymore was fined a record £20,000 by Evans and it looked like the end of his Liverpool career again.

But once again he made his peace, got back in the side and started playing well - well enough this time to work his way into Glenn Hoddle's squad – albeit the depleted one that faced Mexico in March.

The striker deserved a second bite at the England cherry after being discarded by Terry Venables after just two games, both of them in the Umbro Cup competition in June 1995. He's a blend of skill and strength that is rare in a player – he's got enough physical presence to shrug-off challenges from defenders and enough nous to do something clever with the ball afterwards. He's got a sure eye for goal and, when he feels like it, he does a tremendous amount of running off the ball. In short, he's a high quality striker who will probably set the world alight at Villa – until November anyway!

"He's got everything and he's still learning the game."

Frank Clark,
Manager, Nottingham Forest

Vital Statistics

Age 27

Date of Birth 29.5.70

Place of Birth Schaffhausen, Switzerland

League Games & Goals
- Schaffhausen [Switzerland]
- FC Zurich [Switzerland]
- Aarau [Switzerland]
- Lazio [Italy]
- Chelsea 34 [7]

Honours
- Swiss Championship [1993]
- Swiss Player of the Year [1993]
- FA Cup [1997]

Transfers
- Schaffhausen to FC Zurich
- FC Zurich to Aarau
- Aarau to Lazio [£550,000]
- Lazio to Chelsea [£4.5m]

Position/Role
Looking cool and continental, just like the rest of the Chelsea team in fact

Word most often used to describe him
Di-namite

Word never used to describe him
Di-abolical

> "At first I was lonely but now I feel at home."
>
> *Roberto Di Matteo*

Roberto DI MATTEO

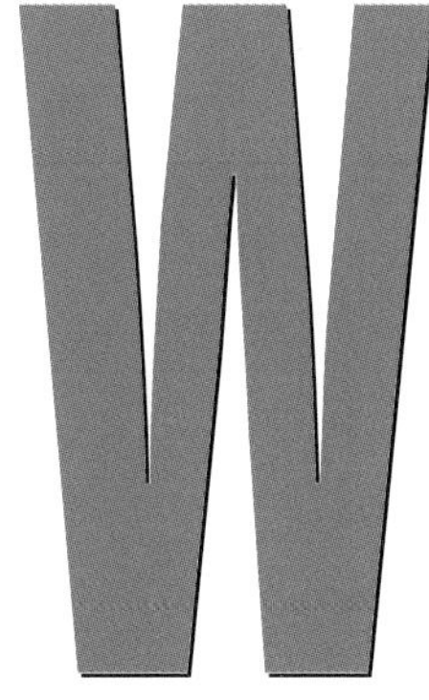

When it was announced that Roberto di Matteo was leaving Lazio to join Chelsea for £4.5 million last year, there were riots in Rome. Although not many people in this country had heard of him at the time, after just one home game in the Premiership, Chelsea fans started to understand just why. Di Matteo - who was the first current Italian international to stop playing in the country – scored a scorching goal which was only bettered by his (and his team-mates) indulgent celebration of it afterwards.

If Roy Hodgson had had his way, the midfielder with the cheeky grin would have been playing for Switzerland instead of Italy. Di Matteo was brought up in the country of cuckoo clocks and cheese with holes in it (though his parents were Italian), and started his playing career there for first division club Aarau. Then, Swiss manager Hodgson fancied him for the World Cup in the USA in 1994, but the midfielder preferred to chance his arm on a place in the Italian team.

Pretty soon after that, Lazio snapped him up for a mere £500,000, and within a year international manager Arrigo Sacchi had called him up. He is now a mainstay in the side and played a significant part in Italy's 1-0 raid on Wembley earlier this year.

Di Matteo has relished his new further-upfront midfield role under Gullit and has demonstrated himself to be a skillful forward threat with excellent passing technique, as well as a good tackler. He's got an eye for the quick 'one-two' and shooting skills that have brought him a number of crucial goals for the Blues with either foot. He is a vital midfield cog when Chelsea are in possession and a quick-route channel into the opposing area when they attack on the break.

Di Matteo has acclimatised well to the English way of life, and showed his instant understanding of the vernacular after his Chelsea debut against Southampton, when he upset a young opposition fan by writing the second strongest taboo word in the language on his hat! It was a stupid thing to do and he was forced to make an apology and fined. Since then, he has hardly put a foot wrong – on or off the pitch.

Coors

Vital Statistics

Age 32

Date of Birth 27.1.65

Place of Birth Newcastle under Lyme

League Games & Goals
Port Vale 294 [77]
Wimbledon 202 [48]

Transfers
Port Vale to Wimbledon [£775,000]

Robbie Earle's 1996/97 season
A crucial and consistent midfield force as the Dons fought for glory on all three fronts. His form brought him to within a whisker of the England squad

Position/Role
Tearing from box to box and arriving late in the opposition's area to terrorise Premiership defences

Word most often used to describe him
Cap-less

Word never used to describe him
International

> "Ever since I've been here we've always got the ball into the box..."
>
> *Robbie Earle*

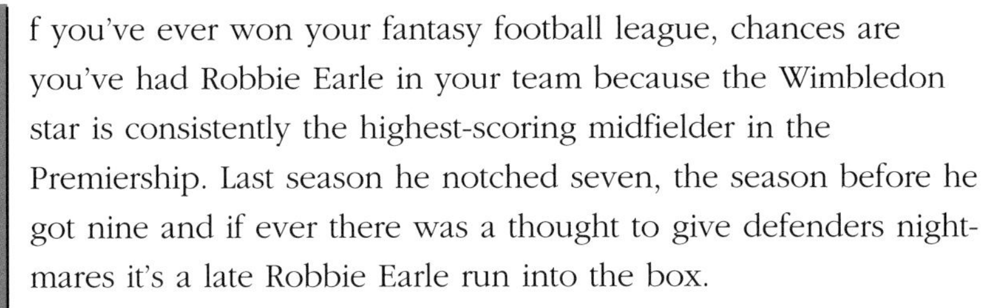

If you've ever won your fantasy football league, chances are you've had Robbie Earle in your team because the Wimbledon star is consistently the highest-scoring midfielder in the Premiership. Last season he notched seven, the season before he got nine and if ever there was a thought to give defenders nightmares it's a late Robbie Earle run into the box.

"That's my strength," agrees the player who signed for Wimbledon from Port Vale for £775,000 in 1991 and has scored more than 48 times for the Dons. "Ever since I've been here we've always got the ball into the box which means I've always had chances to score."

Alongside Vinnie Jones, Earle's performances in the centre of midfield last season were one of the major factors in Wimbledon's astonishing, yet ultimately fruitless, season.

And while Earle's scoring ratio has remained fairly constant around the 15 goals a season mark, much has changed at Wimbledon where he is now one of the club's veteran players. Now so much more than the hit and hope, kick and rush team, which was so despised by football purists, thanks to some shrewd tactics and even shrewder signings by Joe Kinnear, the critics are even beginning to say nice things about the way the Dons play football. Unfortunately, it may have come just a little too late for Earle.

Put on standby for Glenn Hoddle's injury-ravaged squad for the World Cup qualifier at home to Italy in February 1997, at 32, Earle looks to have missed the England boat. Kinnear has not been the only one singing his midfield dynamo's praises for years, but it seems the Wimbledon stigma has counted against him.

It is unlikely that Earle is bitter. A quietly-spoken, thoughtful and level-headed player, he intends to pursue a career in the media after he hangs up his boots. He shouldn't be thinking about that just yet though, because with Wimbledon continuing to defy the odds and mix it up at the top with the big boys, there are plenty of headlines still to be written about him – not by him.

Robbie EARLE

ELONEX

Vital Statistics

Age 30

Date of Birth 18.12.66

Place of Birth London

League Games & Goals
QPR 163 [70]
Newcastle 67 [38]

Honours
PFA Player of the Year 1995/96

Transfers
Hayes to QPR [£15,000]
Besiktas, Turkey [loan]
QPR to Newcastle [£6m]

Position/Role
Muscling in on any sniff of goalmouth action, especially when the ball's in the air

Word most often used to describe him
Head-case

Word never used to describe him
Timid

> "If you've got a monster you've got to feed it"
>
> *Kevin Keegan*

Last season was a quiet one for Les Ferdinand. Sidelined with an injury at the start of the year and playing second fiddle to his more glamourous attacking partners Asprilla and Shearer, you could be forgiven for hardly noticing he was there. Apart from the fact that he still managed to notch 20-odd goals for the club, that is.

When Ferdinand first moved to Newcastle, he was the target for almost all of their attacking movements. "If you've got a monster you've got to feed it," said Kevin Keegan at the beginning of the 1995/96 season, as he promptly constructed a side moulded around the big number nine. With Gillespie and Ginola surging down the wings and providing cross after cross for the former QPR man, it wasn't a question of whether he'd score in a match, but how many he'd get.

The arrival of Asprilla in February 1996 changed Newcastle's shape and Ferdinand's goals dried up as more of Newcastle's attacks flowed through the middle of the park. Then came the arrival of Alan Shearer, and it looked like the big man's days might be numbered at the club – especially as he graciously allowed the £15 million man to take over his number nine shirt.

But Ferdinand quickly learned how to play alongside the blond Geordie and the two formed a partnership that was lethal when it was on song – a fact that Glenn Hoddle acknowledged when he played the two alongside one another in the early World Cup qualifiers. Ferdinand rammed home a valuable goal against Georgia to take his England tally to five in 12 matches.

Ferdinand's forte is his immense strength – once he's on the ball he's extremely difficult to knock off – and his ability to defy the laws of physics and hang in the air waiting for crosses mean that he's rarely off the scoresheet for long. He's not half bad at little flicks to team-mates around the edge of the box either.

So although you might have half-forgotten about Ferdinand in all the hoo-hah about his attacking team-mates, opposing defences certainly won't have.

adidas
NEWCASTLE
BROWN ALE
Mitre
ULTIMAX

UMBRO
DANKA

Duncan FERGUSON

Vital Statistics

Age 25

Date of Birth 27.12.71

Place of Birth Stirling

League Games & Goals
Dundee United 77 [28]
Rangers 10 [1]
Everton 74 [20]

Duncan Ferguson's 1996/97 season
Interrupted by injury but by the end of the season he was back to his awesome best. And his neat turn and shot to score against Liverpool showed there is more to his game than headbanging

Honours
FA Cup [1995]

Did you know?
Ferguson scored on his debut for Scotland against Germany with an outrageous overhead kick

Position/Role
Headbutting the ball into the back of the net

Word most often used to describe him
Giant

Word never used to describe him
Gentle

Let's face it, Duncan Ferguson is terrifying. It's scary enough watching him in action from the Goodison Park stands or on Match of the Day so what it must be like for poor Premiership defenders doesn't bear thinking about. OK, they're on good money, but how much would you expect to earn to play 90 minutes against the footballing equivalent of Ghengis Khan?

When Ferguson turned up on loan at Goodison Park three seasons ago with a hard man reputation and a string of suspended sentences and bans, no one knew quite what to expect. They soon found out. When he scored in the 2-0 victory over Liverpool in one of his first games for Everton, no one on the blue side of Merseyside cared. And when it later turned out he'd spent the night before out on the town (including getting arrested for drink driving), his cult status was secured. "Big Fergie likes a few pints, loves to stay out late and chase the birds, and give a bit of lip in training," observed legendary Scottish striker, drinker and womaniser, Jim Baxter. "In my book he's got all the perfect ingredients for a great footballer."

Whether he takes up Baxter's advice on how to structure his training schedule or not, after a season rudely interrupted by a quick stretch at Her Majesty's pleasure following one decimated by injury, this time around 'Big Dunc' can finally put his 'off the pitch' problems behind him. Instead, he can concentrate on terrifying the life out of defenders – legally!

"He's the most frightening player I've seen in the Premiership for a long time," said ex-Everton midfielder, Duncan MacKenzie. And let's face it, you have to feel sorry for the ball (let alone Ferguson's marker), when the big Scotsman thunders in for one of his trademark headers. But don't think that's all there is to his game. Give him an inch of room, in or just outside the box, and you're liable to pay the penalty.

But what does Ferguson himself think of his hard-man image? Is it all a myth? Underneath that rock solid shell is there a soft, fluffy centre? Er, well we were going to ask Ferguson for his thoughts, but apparently he doesn't like speaking to the media and frankly we were too scared to ask!

"He is the most frightening player I've seen in the Premiership..."

Duncan MacKenzie

Tim FLOWERS

Vital Statistics

Age 30

Date of Birth 3.2.67

Place of Birth Kenilworth

League Games & Goals
- Wolves 63
- Southampton 192
- Swindon 7 [loan]
- Blackburn 139

Honours
- FA Premiership [1995]

Transfers
- Wolves to Southampton [£70,000]
- Swindon [loan]
- Southampton to Blackburn [£2.4m]

Position/Role
- Standing in the Blackburn goal, hoping to get noticed

Word most often used to describe him
- Forgotten

Word[s] never used to describe him
- England's no 1

> “He's got all it takes to make a world-class goalkeeper”
>
> *Pat Jennings*

Tim Flowers has suffered. The season before last he had a bad time – a year summed up in one moment when a weak Stan Collymore shot hit an Ewood Park divot just in front of him and sailed past his arms and into the net. The look on Flowers' face, at that moment, said it all.

In the space of the last two seasons, the former Southampton goalkeeper had gone from championship-winning England regular – for a few games under Venables it looked as if Flowers was to be his number one choice ahead of David Seaman – to the forgotten man of football.

After being overtaken by Ian Walker, David 'Dracula' James (scared of crosses!), and even Leeds keeper Nigel Martyn, Tim Flowers must have felt like he'd upset someone up above.

And unfortunately, with managerless Blackburn struggling at the wrong end of the Premiership table for most of last season, there weren't that many people watching him recover his form. Whenever Flowers picked up the papers, he couldn't find anything about his recall to the England squad... until right at the end of the season when Glenn Hoddle could ignore him no longer in favour of the struggling youngsters James and Walker.

And the legendary former Arsenal goalkeeper, Pat Jennings, still believes Flowers can get back to the very top. “He's got all it takes to make a world class goalkeeper,” says Jennings, record cap holder for Northern Ireland. “He's got agility, he's got good hands, he's got anticipation and he reads the game well.”

He's not entirely forgotten, then. Before Kevin Keegan left Newcastle he was rumoured to be on the verge of making a bid for Flowers, and if he remains at Blackburn under Roy Hodgson and Rovers can regain some of the form that made them champions just three seasons ago (thanks in no small part to their goalkeeper), then all may not be lost.

At 30 he's just about reaching his goalkeeping peak. Unfortunately though, so is David Seaman and flavour of the month Nigel Martyn. Get ready for the worst pun in this book, but if Flowers blossoms again he's still got a chance of getting picked (groan!).

CIS
Cooperative Insurance

Reebok
Carlsberg

Vital Statistics

Age 22

Date of Birth 9.4.75

Place of Birth
Liverpool

League Games & Goals
Liverpool 140 [82]

Robbie Fowler's 1996/97 season
Another barnstorming season which included him scoring his 100th overall goal for Liverpool and his first [of many?!] for England

Honours
Coca Cola Cup [1995]

Did you know?
After trying to overturn a penalty decision awarded in his favour against Arsenal, he received a letter from UEFA President Sepp Blatter commending him on his sportsmanship. A few weeks later, he was fined by UEFA for revealing a political message on a T-shirt under his kit!

Position/Role
Scoring goals and grinning cheekily

Word most often used to describe him
Lethal

Word never used to describe him
Inconsistent

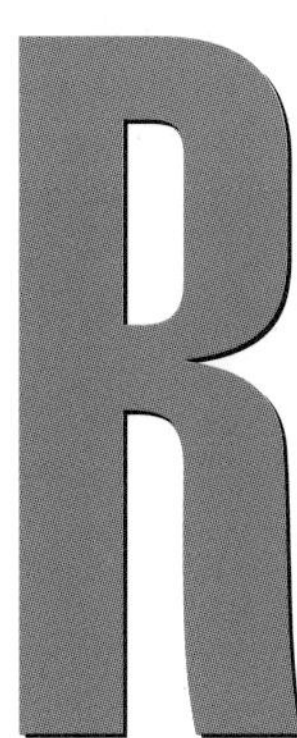

Robbie Fowler is, quite simply, a one-man goalscoring machine. The boy can't stop.

Liverpool legend Graeme Souness, the man who gave Fowler his debut when he was Anfield boss, reckons the 22-year-old hit-man is one in a million. "He could be the greatest they've ever had at Liverpool," says Souness. "Robbie has more natural ability than Ian Rush. Rushie had an incredible ability to sniff out a chance. Fowler has got that too, but also has the ability to take the ball outside the box and do something great."

Last season was incredible even by Fowler's standards. He scored 18 goals in 32 Premiership games. He scored with headers and volleys, tap-ins and long range piledrivers. He scored his first goal for England, and he even tried to turn down a penalty awarded in his favour before managing to get himself sent off just before the crucial end of season run-in. Yes, it was quite a year!

The way Robbie Fowler plays, who'd be a goalkeeper? Aston Villa's Mark Bosnich is just glad he doesn't have to face him every week and rates him ahead of Alan Shearer as the goalkeepers union's most feared opponent.

"He often shoots early, doesn't mind where he shoots from and seems to get late fade on his shots like a golfer," says Bosnich. "But the main reason he scores so many is less complicated. He usually gets ten out of ten shots on target, and with nine out of ten he'll hit the corners. His accuracy is quite amazing."

The only thing that can stop Fowler reaching the very top would seem to be his attitude, and despite the odd blip – like his end of season punch-up with Everton's David Unsworth – unfortunately for Bosnich and his goalkeeping comrades, there doesn't seem to be too much to worry about there either.

"You've got to have a certain arrogance to be a good player, but Robbie's no big-head," says Liverpool coach Ronnie Moran. "There's so much going on in the heads of these young players, especially if they become superstars, and some can handle it and some can't. Robbie can."

> "He could be the greatest they've ever had at Liverpool"
>
> *Graeme Souness*

Ryan Giggs

Vital Statistics

Age 23

Date of Birth 29.11.73

Place of Birth Cardiff

Nickname Er, Giggsy

Appearances and goals
Manchester United 103 [39]

Ryan Giggs' 1996/97 season
Maybe not as spectacular as previous campaigns, but probably - when fit - he was twice as effective. Disappointingly only scored twice in the league, however

Honours
Premiership title [1993, 1994, 1996 and 1997]
FA Cup [1994 and 1996]
League Cup 1992

Position/Role
Breaking the hearts of young girls and defenders alike with his lethal runs

Word most often used to describe him
Genius

Word never used to describe him
Average

> "One day they might even say I was another Ryan Giggs!"
>
> *George Best*

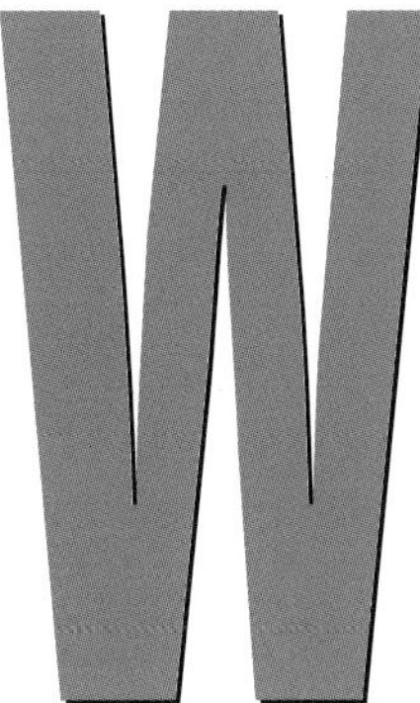hen a tricky new winger starts catching the eye in the Manchester United youth team nowadays, they don't say, "Wow, he could be the new George Best!", they say, "Wow, he could be the new Ryan Giggs!" And as Best himself says, "One day they might even say I was another Ryan Giggs!"

At just 23 years of age, Ryan Giggs is already an Old Trafford legend. And as a veteran of five seasons in United's first team, he's now the wise old man in Fergie's team of fledglings.

Despite the best attempts of the tabloids, he's proved he has what it takes in the brain department to keep his life in order, as well as what he has in his feet to leave opposition defences in tatters. He's overcome the worst injury problems of his career and come back better than ever. At the end of last season his form was awesome. He still has the pace and trickery that once prompted a £10 million bid from AC Milan (whose coach Fabio Capello said, "Like George Best, he has that special fantasia about him"), but he's added the maturity and consistency that turns a good player into a great one.

Now he would cost double what AC Milan bid, but Giggs – the son of a Welsh rugby league player – says he's 'going nowhere'. And that's music to the ears of Alex Ferguson, though probably not the defenders of the Premiership. It's a terrifying thought for them, but young Ryan still has a few years before he reaches his peak.

George Best agrees. "Ryan is really buzzing at the moment, and when you see the kind of stuff he's producing now, what will he be performing like in four or five years time? It really is an exciting and mouthwatering prospect."

Well that's probably the first time for a few years you've seen Ryan Giggs described as an 'exciting prospect'. "You reach your peak around the age of 27," says Best (who incidentally left United aged 26), "and you just wonder what he'll be achieving then." Perhaps he'll have started skipping training, drinking champagne, and dating a string of mystery blondes just like Besty!

UMBRO

SHARP

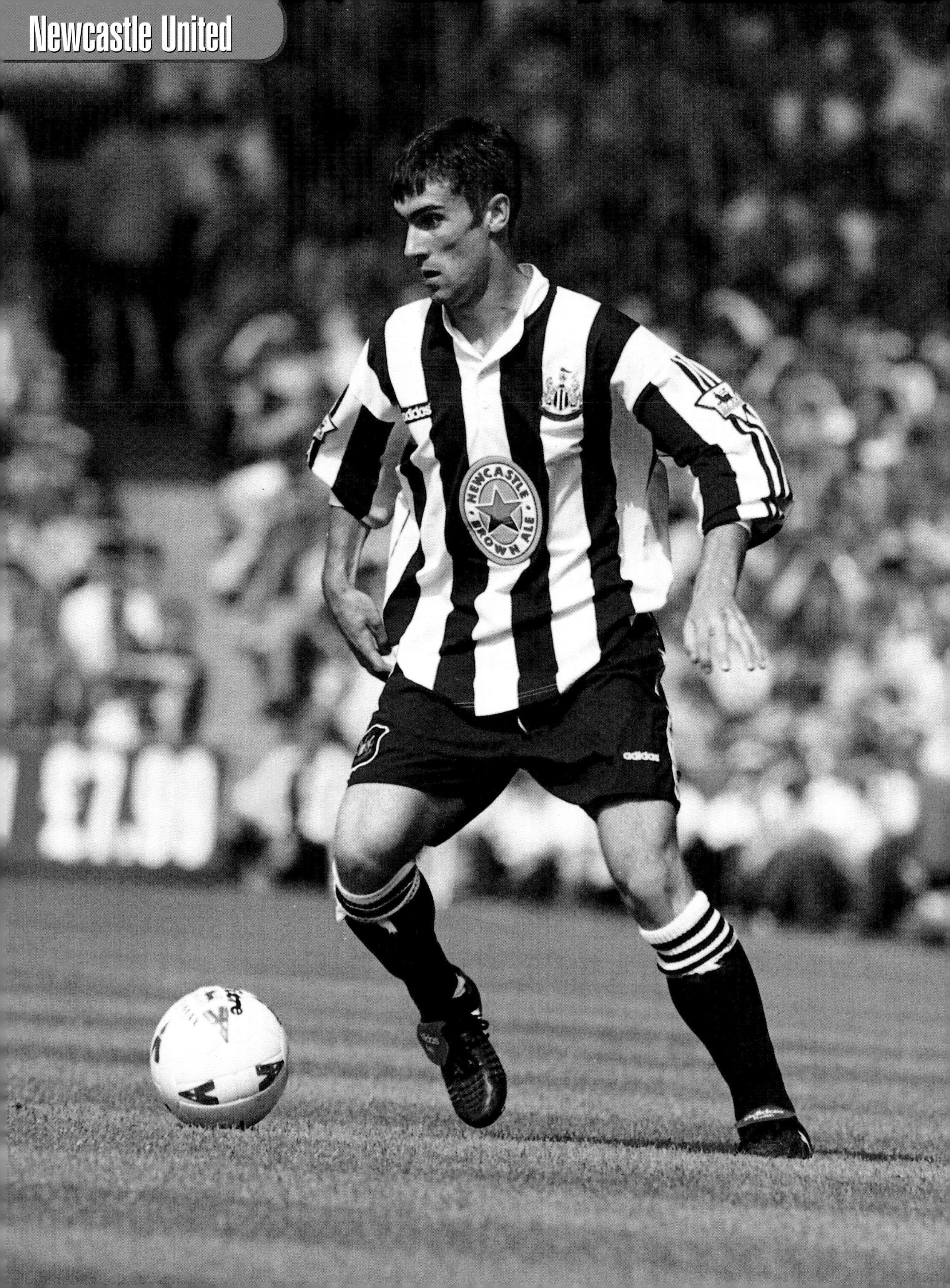
NEWCASTLE
BROWN ALE
adidas
adidas

Vital Statistics

Age 22

Date of Birth 18.2.1975

Place of Birth
Larne, Northern Ireland

League Games & Goals
Wigan 8 [4]
Manchester United 8 [1]
Newcastle United 75 [6]

Transfers
Man Utd to Wigan [loan]
Man Utd to Newcastle [part of Andy Cole transfer, valued at £1m]

Did you know?
Keith Gillespie's first ever league goal was for Man Utd in 1994... against Newcastle

Position/Role
Tearing defences apart or tearing his hair out on the bench

Word most often used to describe him
Lightning

Word never used to describe him
Regular

Perhaps more than any other player in the Premiership, Keith Gillespie is having to get used to the fact that modern football is a squad game.

Despite impressing nearly every time he dons the famous black and white stripes, with a forward line that has included Alan Shearer, Les Ferdinand, Faustino Asprilla and David Ginola, it's not surprising that in the two-and-a-half seasons since he was the less famous part of Andy Cole's transfer, he has become just as familiar with the St James' Park bench as he has with the wings where, when unleashed, he can reap such havoc.

A victim more of differing systems than wavering form, when he's tearing into defences Gillespie always looks a threat. It's a threat that was recognised by Kevin Keegan, and he knew when he received that famous sum of '£6 million plus Keith Gillespie' in 1995, that he certainly wasn't getting ripped off.

When Newcastle surged into a 12-point lead at the top of the Premiership table the following season – a lead which owed no small part to Gillespie's service to lethal Les Ferdinand while Andy Cole looked like a lost lamb at Old Trafford – Fergie might have been ruing the decision to let him go.

But things changed with the arrival of Faustino Asprilla. The 'rubber man' was brought to give the final impetus to Newcastle's surge to the title, but effectively his presence erased Gillespie's name from the teamsheet and the service to Ferdinand dried up. "If you've seen the way I play then you know it is an advantage to me to have a winger in the team," said Les Ferdinand while on England duty. To this day, Newcastle fans look back on Gillespie's absence as the reason why Newcastle let the biggest lead in the history of the Premiership slip.

With Alan Shearer now on the books too, it's hard to know how Kenny Dalglish can accommodate all his big name forwards in the long term. While Keith Gillespie may be the least exotic of those big names you just get the feeling he holds the key...

"It's an advantage to me to have him in the team."

Les Ferdinand

Vital Statistics

Age **19**

Date of Birth **11.1.78**

Place of Birth **Leicester**

Nickname **Bruno**

League Games & Goals
Leicester City 66 [17]

International record
Called up to the England U21 squad last season, now has three caps under his belt

Did you know?
Heskey is so versatile he has been used by Martin O'Neill as an emergency left back

Position/Role
Putting his head down and charging at defenders, just daring them to even try and knock him off the ball

Word most often used to describe him
Heavyweight

Word never used to describe him
Skinny

“...we couldn't have done without him.”

Martin O'Neill

Emile HESKEY

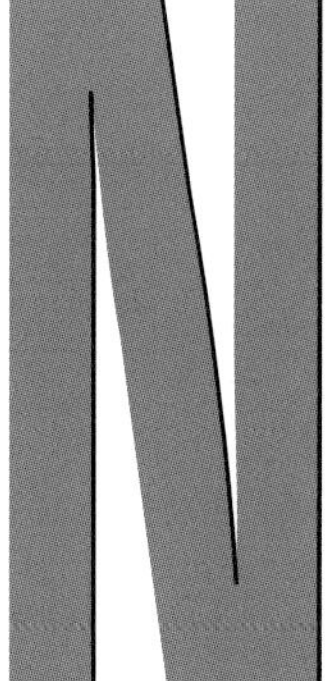

No one at Filbert Street bothers calling Emile Heskey by his real name. He's simply known as 'Bruno'. Young he may be, but the first thing you notice about the 19-year-old Leicester City striker is his heavyweight boxer's shoulders.

“Other boys of his age might be as good technically,” explains City's youth team coach David Nish, “but he has the ability to cope physically as well.”

Heskey's strength has been instrumental in the recent rise of Leicester City under Martin O'Neill. Brought in during the 1994/95 season by necessity (he was still a 16-year-old YTS trainee when he made his debut), the man who went to the same school as Lineker and played for Leicester Boys has hardly looked back since.

“When I first came to the club I thought I might be able to use Emile now and again,” says O'Neill, referring to the 1995/96 promotion season. “In the end, we couldn't have done without him.”

Last season, Heskey was called into the England U21 squad after impressing Glenn Hoddle during a Premiership game against Southampton. Hoddle had gone to the game to check on the form of Matt Le Tissier but came away mesmerised by the Leicester striker who had scored twice, including one of the best goals scored at Filbert Street in living memory. Heskey already had England experience though, having helped the England youth team to third place in the 1995 European Championships in France.

Things could have been very different for Heskey (and Leicester) if David Nish hadn't converted him from a defender into a striker in his mid-teens. Nish believed his pace and power would be better suited to going forward, although at times over the last couple of seasons he has filled-in for Leicester all over the pitch, including left back. When he runs at defenders though, the decision to play him up front is clearly vindicated. Forget Bruno – when Heskey's charging towards them they probably feel it's more like Tyson coming at them!

Mitre
WALKERS
CRISPS

ULTIMAX

Darren HUCKERBY

Vital Statistics

Age 21

Date of Birth 23.4.76

Place of Birth
Nottingham

League Games & Goals
Lincoln City 28 [5]
Newcastle United 1 [0]
Coventry City 25 [5]

Darren Huckerby's 1996/97 season
From the doldrums at Newcastle to heaven at Coventry. All he asked for was a chance, and the lightning-quick winger took it with both hands

Transfers
Lincoln City to Newcastle [£500,000]
Newcastle to Coventry [£1m]

Position/Role
Accelarating past defenders at the speed of light

Word most often used to describe him
Nippy

Word never used to describe him
Sluggish

It was a classic situation – Coventry, deep in the relegation zone mire and without a win since the first day of the season, taking on championship-chasing Newcastle United at Highfield Road last November. Newcastle boasted the attacking talents of Shearer, Ferdinand, Beardsley, Ginola and Gillespie; Coventry were looking to Dion Dublin and a raw teenager named Darren Huckerby.

A month hadn't passed since Huckerby had left Newcastle for Coventry himself, with £1 million going the other way up the M1. Keegan had let the young Nottingham-born winger go exactly because of his strength in depth up front. Whoops. Bad decision!

After six minutes, the blond speed merchant (holding the cuffs of his sleeves like Denis Law), surged through the square Newcastle defence to drill the ball past Srnicek for Coventry's first first-half home goal of the season. Half an hour later, the teenager skipped to the bye-line and weighted a perfect ball back to his skipper, McAllister, who whomped home the Sky Blues' second. It was enough to secure three precious points.

It was poetic justice for Huckerby, who had hardly had a run-out in the year he spent at St. James' Park. Keegan had bought him for £500,000 from Lincoln City, where he had become something of a local hero for his Linford Christie-like pace. Huckerby was on the team coach heading up the motorway for an Auto-Windscreens clash with Darlington, when he was handed the director's mobile phone. Would he be interested in moving to Newcastle United? Of course he would.

Keegan didn't waste much time getting Huckerby a run-out – within a month he came off the bench against Chelsea – but his opportunities at the club were limited. So when Coventry came in after he'd spent a loan spell at Millwall, he didn't have to think too hard about saying "yes".

"He's a keen lad," says Newcastle coach Chris McMenemy. "He's confident to come and ask things and he listens to people." His main strength, however, is something he didn't need to learn about – Huckerby's just about the fastest thing on two legs in the Premiership, as any opposing full-back will tell you after ninety minutes marking him – after he's got his breath back!

> "He's a keen lad. He's confident to come and ask things and he listens..."
>
> *Chris McMenemy*

hp

Vital Statistics

Age 20

Date of Birth 10.11.76

Place of Birth Oslo, Norway

League Games & Goals
Nationalkam [Norway]
Astur [Norway]
Rosenborg [Norway]
Tottenham 16 [6]

International record
Iversen has, at the time of writing, appeared for the Norwegian U21 team on 17 occasions

Iversen's 1996/97 season
After making his debut for Spurs against Coventry City in December he started brightly, faded but then came back with a vengeance only to finish the season on the treatment table

Word most often used to describe him
Flourishing

Word never used to describe him
Cocky

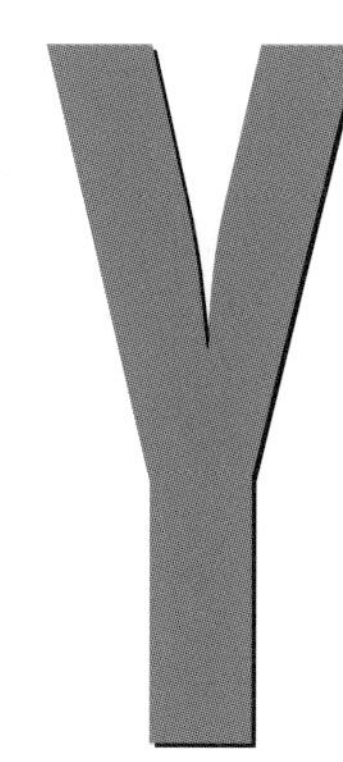

You might think that Norwegian football's most expensive player - a lethal striker chased by Ajax, Barcelona, PSV Eindhoven, Manchester United and Liverpool before he chose to come to Tottenham – might be a bit cocky. You'd be wrong. In fact, Steffen Iversen is one of the shyest players in football.

When he was in negotiation with Tottenham over his £2.6 million move from Norwegian champions Rosenborg last season, it was his mum who did the talking! Apparently his mother, Bente, thought he should be getting a bigger fee on signing. When he arrived in north London, Spurs boss Gerry Francis was worried that his striker was suffering from a crisis of confidence, so he sat him down and showed him a video of all his goals over the previous 18 months.

"He left the room with a big smile on his face," recalls Francis. And it certainly did the trick. The following game, away to Sunderland, he scored a hat-trick although he was too shy to go and ask the referee for the match ball.

Iversen, of course, has nothing to be shy about. Having just turned 20, it was his displays in last season's Champions League – in which Rosenborg beat and knocked out the mighty AC Milan – which had all of Europe's top clubs chasing him. Tottenham, however, had already made contact after Gerry Francis saw him star for the Norwegian Under 21 side. He wined and dined Iversen, and his parents, invited him to visit Spurs and eventually won the race.

And once Iversen agreed to sign for Spurs, he immediately stepped into the number 18 shirt worn by another famous Tottenham import, Jürgen Klinsmann. Being compared with other players isn't anything new for Iversen though, his father – whose name is Odd (seriously!) – was also a famous Rosenborg striker and is Norway's sixth highest goalscorer of all time.

"My father is a legend back in Norway and I have spent my whole life in his shadow," says Iversen the younger. "I have spent my whole life being compared to others and I don't want to any more. I am Steffen Iversen, I am my own player." And most Premiership defenders will already testify to that.

> "My father is a legend back in Norway and I have spent my whole life in his shadow..."
>
> *Steffen Iversen*

Vital Statistics

Age 32

Date of Birth 5.1.65

Place of Birth Watford

Nickname Psycho

League games & goals
Wimbledon 77 [9]
Leeds Utd 46 [5]
Sheff Utd 35 [2]
Chelsea 42 [4]
Wimbledon 152 [12]

International record
Jones has now played for Wales more than ten times, captaining them on three occasions

Honours
FA Cup [Wimbledon] 1988
First Division title [Leeds] 1990

Word most often used to describe him
Committed

Word never used to describe him
Shy

> "...there's more to football than roaring about like a chicken with no head"
>
> *Vinnie Jones*

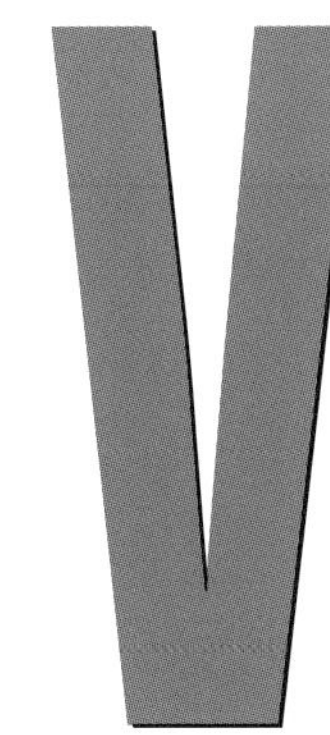innie Jones picks up the ball midway inside the Manchester United half. He stops, looks up, and tucks a perfect ball between two defenders and into the path of Wimbledon teammate, Marcus Gayle. Goal! No, this isn't one of Sam Hammam's psychedelic dreams, you've just met the new, improved Vinnie Jones.

"Since working with Joe Kinnear and being picked for Wales, I've realised that there's more to football than roaring about like a chicken with no head," says the man they've called 'psycho' at every club he's played for. "I know my enthusiasm, aggression and fitness are my strengths," says Jones, "but Joe likes us to play the ball about, to link up the play, and I've tried to polish myself up a bit. But I don't expect to get any credit. I only care what Joe Kinnear and Bobby Gould think, the rest can sod off."

Vinnie himself may be sodding off, having taken court action against Wimbledon over 'freedom of contract'. He has always claimed he never wanted to leave the Dons, but took the action to strengthen his hand in getting an improved contract. If he could get one as improved as his football playing, then he'd be a happy man.

It's all a long way from non-league Wealdstone where Jones began his footballing career whilst working as a builder. The most famous 'former hod carrier' in football made his debut for Dave Bassett's Wimbledon in 1987, when the gang was more demented than crazy, and it wasn't long before he was treading the now familiar route to the FA for disciplinary hearings.

Sent off 12 times in his nine-year career with Wimbledon, Chelsea and Leeds (although under Howard Wilkinson he was never dismissed), Vinnie now says he's grown up and learned a few lessons, although he's still the man the Premiership fans love to hate.

"I just get on with it, but the abuse does get me down sometimes," says Jones. "Most players don't know the kind of stress I get, the kind of stress people like Cantona get, and I give myself a pat on the back for the way I've handled it."

Whatever the outcome of his proposed court action, one thing is for sure – the Premiership would be a duller place without Vinnie Jones. And (whisper it quietly) the boy can play a bit too!

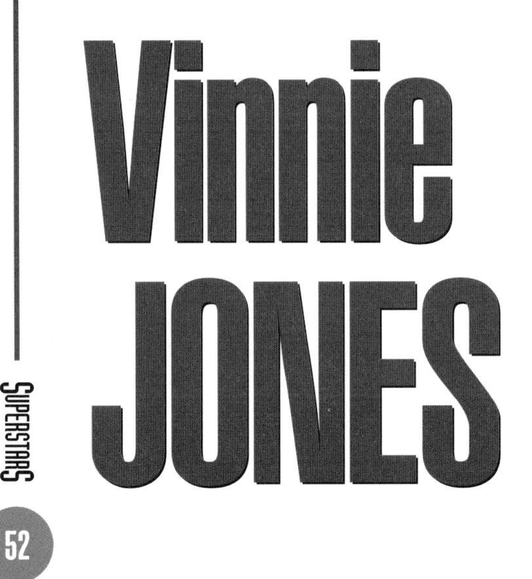

Lotto
ELONEX

Vital Statistics

Age **26**

Date of Birth **10.8.71**

Place of Birth **Cork**

Nickname **Keano**

League Games & Goals
Nottingham Forest 114 [22]
Manchester United 112 [16]

Roy Keane's 1996/97 season
A colossus at the heart of United's title-winning midfield, only when Keane was in the side did the Reds truly look at their best

Honours
Premiership [1994, 1996 and 1997]
FA Cup [1994 and 1996]

Position/Role
Running midfield and trying not to get too angry

Word[s] most often used to describe him
Full blooded

Word never used to describe him
Wimp

couple of seasons ago, Roy Keane was said to be tailor-made to fill Paul Ince's boots. Now arguably the most complete footballer in England, last season he turned out to be tailor-made to fill the boots of just about any United legend you care to mention. Either filling in as a central defender in place of departed skipper Steve Bruce, standing in for David Beckham on the right or Ryan Giggs on the left, he was outstanding. And, of course, whenever Eric Cantona was having an off day, he'd step up and knock in a goal or two as well.

Keane may indeed have been tailor-made to fill Ince's boots. Like Ince though, the 26-year-old Irishman took a while to settle into a rhythm at Old Trafford and has sometimes taken the 'battling' qualities of his game too literally. But apart from when the red mist rises (usually closely followed by the red card rising), when he's playing in his favoured position, Keane is the driving force behind United's mid-field. One moment he's providing a platform for the likes of Giggs and Cantona with his hard-running, hard-tackling, never-say-die spirit, the next he's able to break forward with super skill and deadly awareness. And he doesn't like losing either. "The gaffer wouldn't have any of us in the team if we didn't have that spirit," says Keane. "It's all right being skillful, but you've got to have the will to win. After all, that's the whole point of the game." The irony is, off the pitch, the lad from County Cork is one of the mildest mannered players in the whole Manchester United squad. And over the years he's already calmed down plenty. Nowadays, he nips down his local every now and again instead of spending every night out on the town.

It's worked. Highly respected Dons' manager, Joe Kinnear, claims Keane is the best player in the Premiership and admits he dreams of seeing him playing one day for Wimbledon (maybe as the captain of the Dublin Dons!). But for the moment the Irish international is staying put. Despite the opportunity to earn a small fortune by moving to any of Europe's top clubs under the Bosman ruling, Keane has signed a new contract that'll keep him at Old Trafford until the year 2000. He says, "If I'd been at any other English club I think I would've definitely left. This place is different. United is as big as anywhere."

> "It's all right being skillful, but you've got to have the will to win... that's the whole point..."
>
> *Roy Keane*

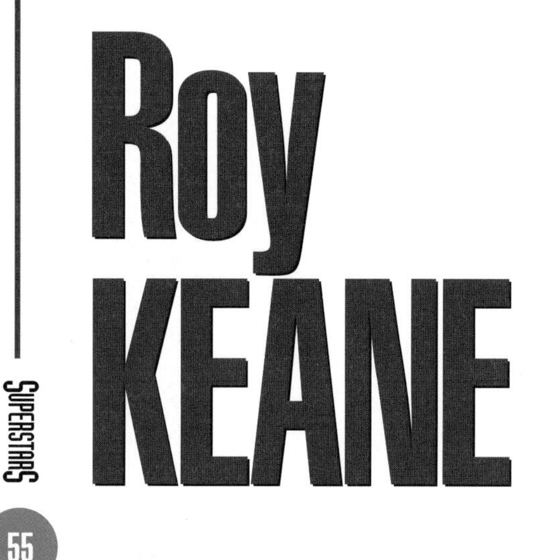

Vital Statistics

Age 29

Date of Birth 17.10.68

Place of Birth Jersey

Nickname
Rag [after the number plate on his old car]

League Games & Goals
Chelsea 90 [8]
Blackburn 128 [5]

Graeme Le Saux's 1996/97 season
A glorious return to the fray, regaining his Blackburn place and then returning to the fold for England

Honours
Premiership [1995]

Did you know?
Before being injured, Graeme had played in every England game under Terry Venables

Position/Role
Thrusting down the left with his hair tufting up in the wind

Word most often used to describe him
Back

Word never used to describe him
Lucky

> "I always dreamed of playing for England again"
>
> *Graeme Le Saux*

The Manchester United physio has a picture of Graeme 'Tintin' Le Saux on his surgery wall. Underneath the picture he has scrawled a caption which reads, 'This is a man in pain.' The picture was taken just after the Blackburn wing-back horrifically injured his ankle in a game against Middlesbrough in December 1995.

"I could see my heel where my foot should have been," remembers Le Saux of the incident that twisted his foot round nearly 180 degrees. "Then the pain arrived."

It was the end of a nightmare month for the Jersey-born defender, who had been fined £10,000 for punching his teammate David Batty during a Champions League clash against Russian title-holders, Spartak Moscow, in November.

And what made Le Saux's pain even worse was that it came after the best season of his life, in which he'd capped off a superb campaign which saw him win the Championship with Blackburn and a regular berth in the England team with a Brazilian-style goal against the Brazilians at Wembley.

1996/97 was much kinder for the Channel-Islander. After a long recuperation period (which saw him miss the European Championship), he finally returned against West Ham in October and his return to the team coincided with a run of form that pushed Blackburn off the bottom of the table and into the security of a mid-table position (although Blackburn fans will tell you it was no coincidence).

What really topped things off for Le Saux was winning his England place back for the vital World Cup qualifier at Wembley against Italy in February 1997. Even though the nippy left-footer wasn't back to the sort of form he was showing for Terry Venables in the build-up to Euro '96, he performed pretty well.

And so he might. He's comfortable on the ball, good at crossing, a fine tackler and has the pace and stamina to roam the wings from box to box without getting caught out of position. In short, he's a natural left-sided wing back. And for Glenn Hoddle, a natural left-sided wing-back is manna from heaven. Le Saux should be in his team for years to come, barring injury of course.

Graeme LE SAUX

asics
CIS
Co-operative Insurance
asics

PONY
PONY

Vital Statistics

Age 28

Date of Birth 14.10.68

Place of Birth Guernsey

Nickname God

League Games & Goals
Southampton 357 [139]

Matt Le Tissier's 1996/97 season
Not a great season for 'Le Tiss', by the end of it he was keeping the bench warm for the Saints. His long-awaited call up for England seemed to come just at the wrong time

Position/Role
Marauding genius who looks like he's pulling a strop... even when he's just scored from 45 yards

Word most often used to describe him
Enigma

Word never used to describe him
Workmanlike

Poor Matt Le Tissier got blamed almost entirely for England's Wembley defeat at the hands of the Italians last February. It was mainly because he fluffed England's best chance to score in the first half before Gianfranco Zola slotted-in Italy's goal. Shortly after, a Le Tissier header – which should have been on target – went wide.
16 minutes later, Stuart Pearce delivered a dream cross for the Channel Islander who was waiting in the box, but for once in his life he needed two touches and by the time he got his shot in, Italian defender Fabio Cannavaro had blocked off the route to goal and the ball ricocheted harmlessly into midfield.

Le Tissier was substituted on the hour to a chorus of boos and the next day most of the scandalrags focused on his failure to deliver. 'Matt is Tisstory' screamed *The Sun*, adding 'You must be taking the Tiss' after Hoddle had stated he would consider picking the Southampton forward again.

"It's not the end of Le Tissier's international career, no way," said Hoddle afterwards, pointing out that at least the number ten had got himself into two scoring positions, which is more than most of the rest of the team managed to do!

Hoddle is the man who picks the team and he's wise not to count the forward out of his plans. Le Tissier is one of the most skillful and intelligent footballers in the Premiership. He has the knack of scoring incredible goals at just the right time – witness his dipping 40-yarder in 1994/95 that caught Blackburn keeper, Tim Flowers, inches out of position and yards away from getting a hand to the ball. It had Motty enthusing, "Only Matt Le Tissier can do that because only he would have thought of it!" Then there was Le Tissier's screaming late equaliser against Newcastle in January 1997 that Kenny Dalglish called a 'wondergoal'.

"He's one of very few players I've seen with all-round ability," drools Alan Ball about his former charge. "He can play it long, he can play it short, he's superbly precise in his passing, he's a magnificent manipulator and he can make and score goals. In short, he's a one-off."

> "He's one of very few players I've seen with all-round ability."
>
> *Alan Ball*

Reebok
Carlsberg

Vital Statistics

Age 25

Date of Birth 11.2.72

Place of Birth Liverpool

Nickname
Macca/Shaggy

League Games & Goals
Liverpool 217 [32]

Honours
FA Cup [1992]
League Cup [1995]

Steve McManaman's 1996/97 season
Played in all but two of Liverpool's 38 league games but, just like Liverpool, faded towards the end of the season

Did you know?
Sir Stanley Matthews once complimented Steve on his 'dribbling'

Position/Role
Trying to beat defenders before he snaps in half

Word most often used to describe him
Mac-nificent

Word never used to describe him
Ordinary

Steve McManaman carries on improving his breathtaking ability to run at and beat defenders at will, his spindly body gyrating wildly and the ball apparently glued to his left foot. This inevitably smacks of the days when shorts were baggy (yes, even baggier than United's current design), and every team had two wingers. But McManaman is not really a winger. His strength is not in beating men, getting to the by-line and firing in crosses, he's at his best when he's skipping past tackles, cutting in from the by-line and going straight for goal.

Handed a free role by Liverpool boss Roy Evans over the last two seasons, McManaman has been on fire. Now an England regular, he's been showing the kind of form in a red, white and blue shirt that he shows every week at Anfield, but this time against the defenders of Italy and Poland, not Derby and Coventry.

Still only 25, McManaman – who made his debut way back in 1990 – has now played more than 200 league games for Liverpool after being snapped up from right under the noses of the Everton scouts as an 11-year-old. Ironic seeing as he was a true blue Everton fan with Bob Latchford and Duncan MacKenzie posters plastered all over his bedroom walls!

"He always had confidence, even then," recalls Liverpool assistant manager, Ronnie Moran. "When you saw him coming down the corridor you'd think, 'Aye, aye, who's this then?'. He walked with a swagger like he does now, but he's no bighead. He's a sensible lad who looks after himself and that's why he's made it."

By the end of the last campaign McManaman was visibly jaded, however. After nearly two years non-stop football - taking into account Euro '96 - maybe it was time for a rest. When he comes back fully refreshed he will know that he has the opportunity to become one of the most influential players ever to play for Liverpool and England.

And despite some great goals for the Reds last season, if there's one area in which McManaman's game could improve, it's his shooting. Premiership defenders will be dismayed to hear, then, that he's planning extra work on his only real weakness. Gulp!

> "He's a sensible lad who looks after himself and that's why he's made it."
>
> *Ronnie Moran*

PUMA
LEEDS UNITED
AFC

Vital Statistics

Age 30

Date of Birth 11.8.66

Place of Birth St Austell

League games
Bristol Rovers 101
Crystal Palace 272
Leeds Utd 36

Nigel Martyn's 1996/97 season
Back in the limelight in the top flight after missing out with Palace in the play-offs, Martyn showed the form of his life, earning gushing praise from manager George Graham and a place in Glenn Hoddle's England squad

Position/Role
Providing the foundations for George Graham's rock-solid Arsenal-like defence with his uncanny [though without moustache], impersonation of David Seaman

Word most often used to describe him
Magnificent

Word never used to describe him
Shaky

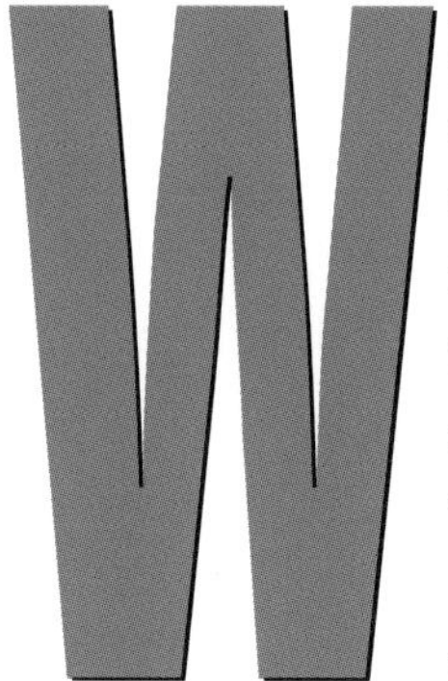

When Nigel Martyn grew a moustache people used to say he was trying to look like David Seaman, so he shaved it off. But it will take more than facial hair trimming to disguise the similarities between the two. Nothing flash, nothing too risky, just good, solid, reliable goalkeeping. Plus the occasional world-class piece of brilliance of course.

And although Seaman is currently England's undisputed number one keeper, Martyn has forced himself into the reckoning with an outstanding first campaign at Leeds United - including more than 20 clean sheets – and by the end of last season he was back in the England set-up.

Martyn had last played for his country against Germany back in 1993 when he was at Crystal Palace, and believes that dropping out of the Premiership with the Eagles damaged his chances no-end. After moving to Leeds for £1 million, following Palace's disappointment in the play-off final, the 30-year-old goalkeeper has been enjoying a new lease of life.

"I've had a fresh challenge and it's really extended me. George Graham has consistently sung my praises. Sometimes that can work against me, that's why I've tended to keep quiet about my form." One person who's not likely to be so reticent is Martyn's goalkeeping coach, John Burridge, the goalkeeping veteran of 18 English league clubs who also works with fellow England star, Tim Flowers.

"I have a little rule," explains Burridge. "I don't get associated with keepers who are not brave and who don't want to do the work. Nigel does, and is in my opinion a tremendous goalkeeper."

And Burridge's coaching seems to be working. After taking over at Leeds, George Graham appeared to launch a 'Martyn for England' campaign every Saturday afternoon in post-match press conferences. When Glenn Hoddle named his squad for the friendly against Mexico in May, Graham got his wish. And with Ian Walker and David James perhaps lacking experience and consistency, Martyn could well be the answer. He could play in place of David Seaman and people wouldn't even notice, which he would take as the highest of compliments.

> "I don't get associated with keepers who don't want to do the work. Nigel does, and is... a tremendous goalkeeper."
>
> *John Burridge*

Paul MERSON

Vital Statistics

Age 29

Date of Birth 20.3.68

Place of Birth London

Nickname Merse

League games & goals
Brentford [loan] 7
Arsenal 327 [78]

Honours
League title [1989 and 1991]
FA Cup [1993]
League Cup [1993]
European Cup Winners' Cup [1994]

Paul Merson's 1996/97 season
Back to his best [maybe even better than his old best] as the new, improved [alcohol and drug free] Paul Merson re-discovered how to enjoy his football

Word most often used to describe him
Resurrected

Word never used to describe him
Dopey

"Merson has a gloss and a sheen about him I haven't seen since he was a teenager."

Ron Atkinson

For Paul Merson, football is the great escape. "When I get out on the pitch I can get away from everything and just play football," he says. "It's more than important to me. It's the ultimate."

Merson has been having a tough time off the pitch recently. Battling on three fronts against addiction to alcohol, cocaine, and gambling and suffering after the break-up of his marriage, Merson has to take every day as it comes and then cope with another one. But when he runs onto the turf, he's been performing like somebody's just recharged his batteries. "Merson has a gloss and sheen about him I haven't seen since he was a teenager," says Ron Atkinson about the attacking midfielder.

The player the Gooners call 'Magic Man' has started to come up trumps every time he pulls on the red and white shirt. And he's added a vital new ingredient to his game that was lacking before he made his comeback after three months rehabilitation in 1996 – consistency. His passes rarely go amiss, his crosses more often than not find their target, his shots rarely threaten the linesmen any more, and he's still able to come up with the moments of inspired genius that have always distinguished him from less gifted Premiership players. He's even won his place in the England squad back.

Merson first appeared on the scene for Arsenal as a cocky 17-year-old who looked like he needed a good few steaks and six months intensive training at the gym. But his career soon blossomed and by the time he notched up his 400th game for Arsenal, he'd scored 100 goals, won an FA Cup, two championships, a League Cup and a European Cup Winners' Cup as well as 15 caps and 1 goal for England.

Arsenal stopped winning trophies around the time that Merson's lifestyle started showing in his game, and as a born again teetotaller he would love to get another piece of silverware on his mantelpiece as a mark of how far he's come since those dark days.

Don't bet against it. But if you do, don't expect to see Merse propping up the counter at the bookies you go to.

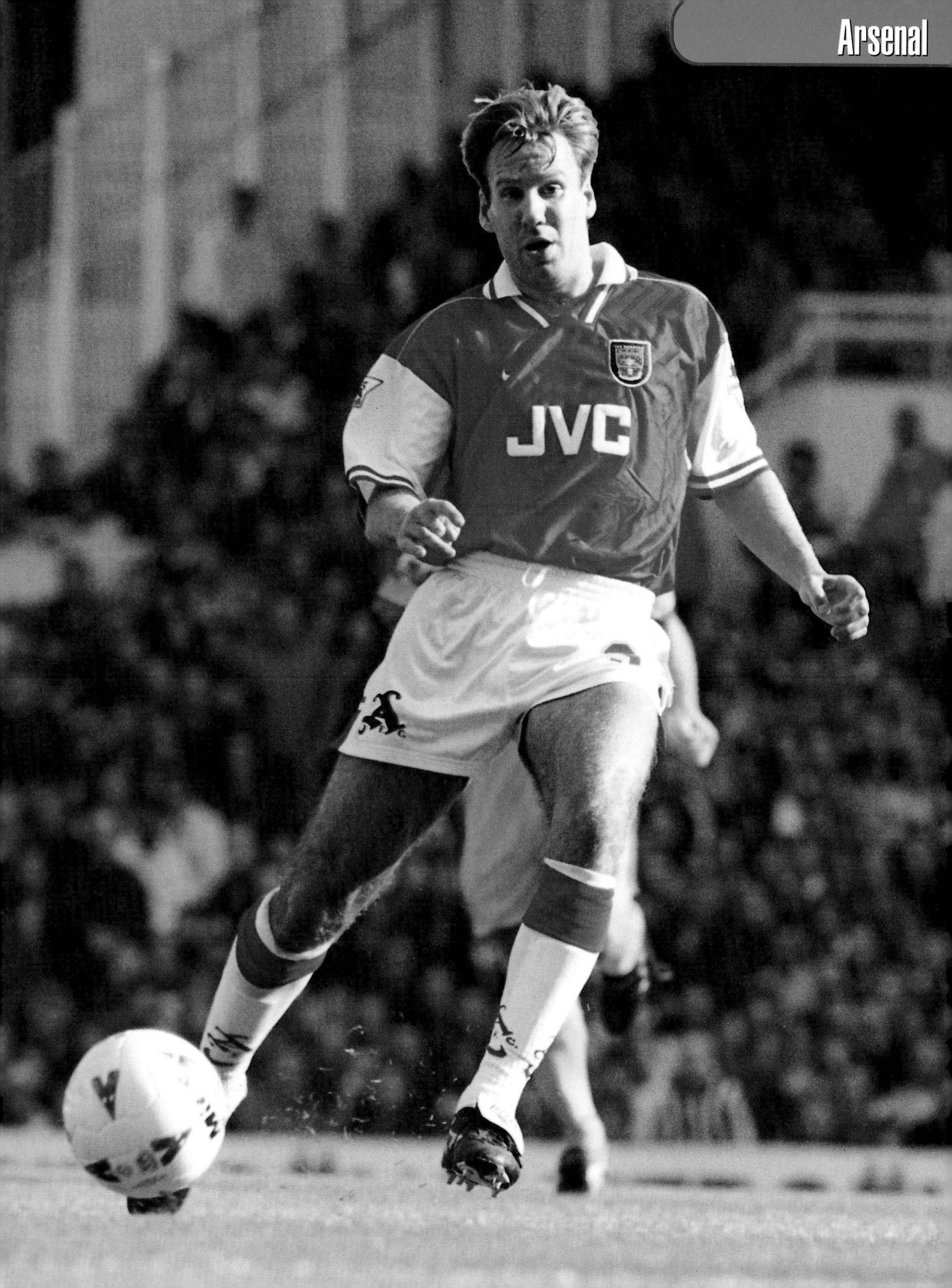
JVC

UMBRO
UMBRO
UMBRO
UMBRO

Peter SCHMEICHEL

Vital Statistics

Age 33

Date of Birth 18.11.63

Place of Birth Glodsone, Denmark

League Games & Goals
Brondby 214
Manchester United 225

Schmeichel's 1996/97 season
As consistent as ever, again a major reason why the Premiership trophy sits proudly on display at Old Trafford

Honours
Danish League [Brondby] [1987, 1988, 1989]
Danish Cup [1989]
Danish Player of the Year [1990]
League Cup [1992]
FA Premiership [1993, 1994, 1996, 1997]
FA Cup [1994 and 1996]
European Championship [Denmark] [1992]

Transfers
Brondby to Man Utd [£550,000]

Position/Role
Looming large in front of the goal – at either end

Word most often used to describe him
Mighty

Word never used to describe him
Quiet

Peter Schmeichel's hold on the unofficial title of 'world's best goalkeeper' is as tight as his grip on the ball whenever it comes within reach of those giant gloves. It helps, of course, that he's playing in front of one of the tightest defences in the Premiership, a defence so wary of a Danish ear-bashing (even when seemingly it's the goalkeepers' fault), that their main motivation in stopping an opponent getting a shot on goal is almost certainly downright fear.

Former United captain Steve Bruce reckons, "it's his way of concentrating," and insists, "Schmeichel is the best I've ever seen." Anyone who saw his incredible Banks-like save against Rapid Vienna in the Champions League last season could hardly argue.

United fans wholeheartedly agree, and since his bargain basement £550,000 move from Brondby in the summer of 1991, he's provided the rock-solid foundations for five years of United success. He is United's best-ever keeper and that's official – statistics show he concedes, on average, one goal every 116 minutes.

How many times last season did the giant Dane keep United in a match? How often was a clean-through striker thwarted by Schmeichel's huge, fluorescent green frame? With hands the size of Jutland, an XXXL-sized frame that swallows-up the goal, and the kind of super-confidence needed to dominate a Premiership penalty area, Schmeichel's got the lot.

But there's more to Schmeichel than shot-stopping. With his colossal 'defence to attack' throws, which Alex Ferguson has described as "like Glenn Hoddle passes," it's like having another midfielder on the pitch. And then there's his goalscoring! As well as his UEFA Cup header against Rotor Volograd the season before last, he scored once in the Danish Third Division as well as in the 1994 Charity Shield penalty shoot-out against David Seaman.

In fact, he'd probably do a better job up front than Andy Cole, but Alex Ferguson knows that having Schmeichel between the sticks is one of the major reasons he's just stuck two big bits of silverware in the Old Trafford trophy cabinet.

Cantona might get the adulation while Giggsy and Beckham get the groupies. Schmeichel just goes out and gets United results.

> "Schmeichel is the best that I have ever seen."
>
> *Steve Bruce*

Vital Statistics

Age 33

Date of Birth 19.9.63

Place of Birth Rotherham

League games & goals
Peterborough Utd 91
Birmingham City 75
QPR 141
Arsenal 249

David Seaman's 1996/97 season
Interrupted by injury, and oh how England missed him against Italy

Honours
League Championship [1991]
FA Cup [1993]
League Cup [1993]
European Cup Winners Cup [1994]

Position/Role
Saving the day for Arsenal, usually

Word most often used to describe him
Safe

Word never used to describe him
Flamboyant

> “I was the proudest man in England during Euro '96.”
>
> *David Seaman*

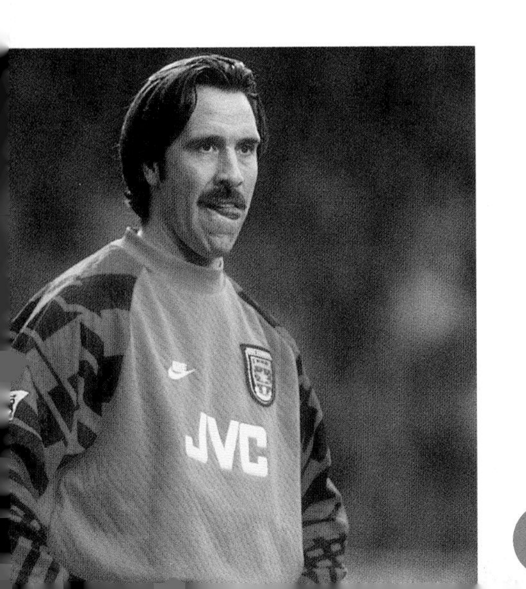

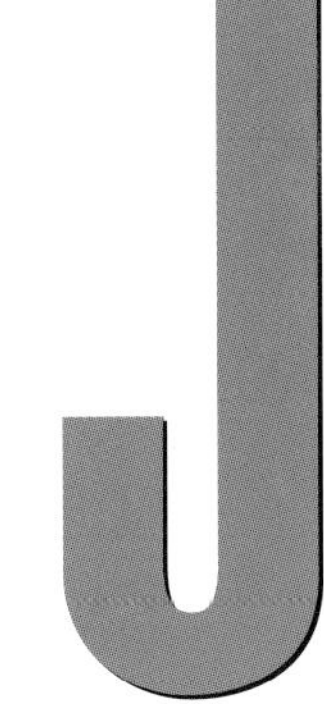

ust after Euro '96 last summer, David Seaman decided to pay a visit to Wimbledon to watch the tennis. As he quietly made his way to his seat, he suddenly realised that the entire centre court crowd was on its feet, cheering, clapping and looking at him. "It was," he says, "a total shock. Completely unexpected."

Seaman's heroic, nation-uniting performances in that tournament – including two crucial penalty saves against Scotland and then in the quarter final shoot-out against Spain – were more predictable. If there's one thing that seems to remain consistent in the funny old game of football, it's that David Seaman is just about the most reliable goalkeeper in the world.

Okay, so there was 'Nayim from the halfway line' in the 1995 European Cup Winners' Cup Final, a rare blunder as the former Spurs man's lob sailed over his head, but can you recall another? "It was the worst moment of my career," admits Seaman, "but it's how you handle the mistakes that is vital and I'm stronger in mind and body now."

Seaman's career didn't start too well either. Rejected by Leeds United where he was an apprentice, he moved to Peterborough, Birmingham and then QPR before Arsenal offered him his big break, smashing the British transfer record for a goalkeeper by forking out £1.3 million for him in 1990.

Replacing crowd favourite John Lukic, the Arsenal fans were unsure of him at first, but when he conceded just 18 goals in his first season (in which the Gunners won the title), they soon took him to their hearts. Now, of course, he's a hero to all England not just the red and white half of north London.

"I was the proudest man in England during Euro '96 – proud to be part of a team giving the country such a lift and proud to do well and make saves. It doesn't matter how good a player you are, you think you are, or people say you are, it's only when you prove it in a major tournament that you can expect to be regarded as world class. I went into the finals as England's number one and was determined to be the best in the world. That was my ambition."

And there are plenty who'd say it is one he's achieved.

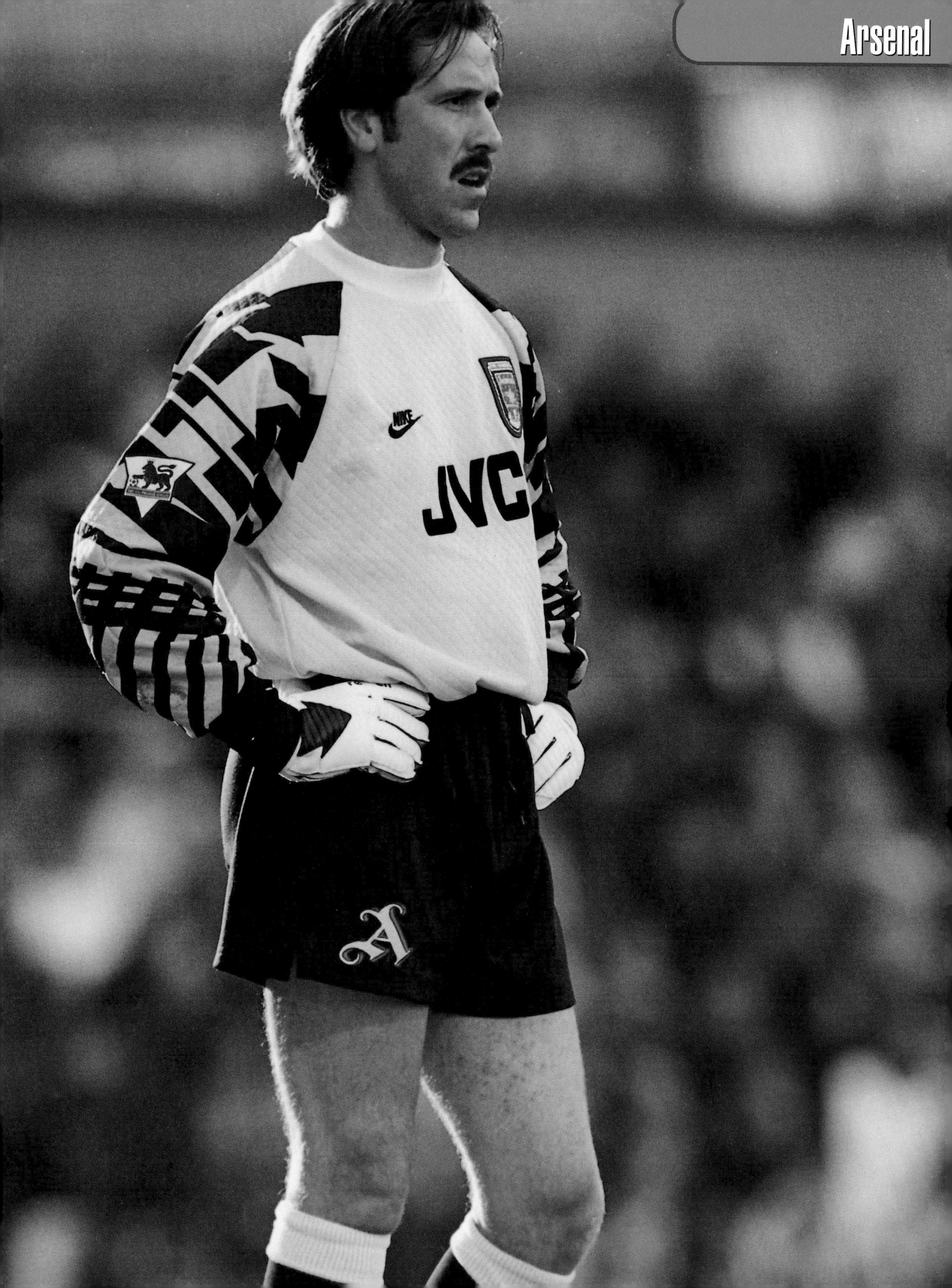
NIKE
JVC

adidas
NEWCASTLE BROWN ALE
adidas

Vital Statistics

Age 27

Date of Birth 13.8.70

Place of Birth Newcastle

League Games & Goals
Southampton 118 [23]
Blackburn 140 [112]
Newcastle 30 [25]

Alan Shearer's 1996/97 season
Spent the season banging them in as usual, this time in the black and white stripes of his hometown club

Honours
Premiership title [1995]

Transfers
Southampton to Blackburn [£3.6m]
Blackburn to Newcastle [£15m]

Did you know?
Alan Shearer is the youngest ever top flight hat-trick scorer. He scored three on his debut for Southampton v Arsenal, aged just 17

Position/Role
Scoring goals like it's going out of fashion

Word most often used to describe him
Relentless

Word never used to describe him
Cheap

World's most expensive player, England captain, Player of the Season (again!) – how long before we have to start calling him 'Sir Alan Shearer'? 'Obscene' screamed some newspaper headlines when Shearer's record breaking £15 million transfer to Newcastle United was announced last August, but pretty much everyone else knows a bargain when they see one.

"If you want a Rolex watch then there are only two ways to get it," said then Newcastle boss, Kevin Keegan, at the time. "Either you steal it or you pay the money it costs."

Shearer repaid Keegan's compliment by stepping into a black and white shirt and carrying on doing what he's done for every team he's ever played for – scoring goals. He scored a hat-trick on his debut for Southampton when he was still only 17, he was top scorer in the Premiership two years in a row for Blackburn, scored on his England debut against France in 1992 and finished as top scorer in Euro '96.

None of which came as any surprise to former Southampton boss, Dave Merrington, who remembers well the first time he saw Shearer unleash that lethal right foot when he was the Saints' youth team manager.

"He could only have been 15 or 16 at the time," Merrington recalls. "We were playing at home when the ball was played to him in the box. He took it on his chest, rolled the defender to his left, the ball dropped and he hit it with his right foot from 30 yards. It went in like a rocket."

Shearer's been doing it ever since, and happily for all Geordies, now he's doing it for his hometown club. They could have got him a tad cheaper though, it has to be said, because when he went for a trial there as a youngster they told him to go in goal!

That's all water under the bridge now, of course, and if United are to break their trophy voodoo – they haven't won anything for 28 years – you can bet your Toon Army socks it'll be Shearer's goals that do it for them. And if he does, they might just have to erect a statue to him at St James' Park, right next to the one of Jackie Milburn.

> "If you want a Rolex watch then there are only two ways to get it. Either you steal it or you pay the money it costs."
>
> *Kevin Keegan*

Teddy SHERINGHAM

Vital Statistics

Age 31

Date of Birth 2.4.66

Place of Birth Highams Park

League Games & Goals
Millwall 220 [93]
Aldershot [loan] 4 [1]
Nottingham Forest 42 [14]
Tottenham Hotspur 166 [71]

Did you know?
Teddy Sheringham is Millwall's highest scorer of all time

Transfers
Millwall to Aldershot [loan]
Millwall to Nottm Forest [£2.0m]
Forest to Tottenham [£2.1m]

Position/Role
The once, but not anymore, unsung hero of Spurs and England

Word most often used to describe him
Class

Word never used to describe him
Shearer-like

> "He doesn't just have the capacity to score goals – he can make them and he can stop them."
>
> *Garth Crooks*

It wasn't so long ago that everyone, except for a few Tottenham fans, moaned when Teddy Sheringham's name appeared on the England teamsheet. A thousand punters in a thousand pubs lied through their fat bellies that they could go out and do better than him. He wasn't so much an unsung hero as a national joke. But Sheringham plugged away, never let anyone down, and now those same fans moan when they hear he's injured or not playing.

"He certainly deserves his place in the England team," says his Spurs skipper Gary Mabbutt, no stranger to the three-lioned shirt himself and a man who suffers most days at the hands of his wily team-mate in training. "He's come on in leaps and bounds since he joined Tottenham, and he's improving all the time. The thing is, many people don't notice half the work he's doing. His strength is his all-round ability."

It was former Spurs manager, Terry Venables, who made Sheringham his first choice partner for Alan Shearer. Wily old Venables realised that in international football you need forward players with brains as well as brawn, and the equally wily Sheringham became the crucial link between England's midfield and attack.

Tottenham striker, Garth Crooks, explains. "He's a genuine all-round footballer, which is an enormous strength. He doesn't just have the capacity to score goals – he can make them and he can stop them. And most importantly he has presence.

"A defence knows he's there and assumes respect. Martin Chivers had that sort of presence. Greaves had it, Best had it, Gascoigne has it, all the great players have it. It can give you an extra yard because you have respect."

Unlike pub punters and pompous pundits, Premiership defenders have been giving Sheringham respect for years – his 20-plus goals every season in the white shirt of Tottenham have made sure of that. Finally, it looks like England fans are being forced to feel the same way. And about time too!

PONY
HEWLETT
PACKARD

Vital Statistics

Age 24

Date of Birth 26.2.73

Place of Birth
Kristiansund, Norway

League Games & Goals
FK Clausenengen [Norway] 71 [86]
Molde FK [Norway] 40 [31]
Man Utd 31 [17]

Solskjaer's 1996/97 season
Proof that fairytales do come true. Solskjaer arrived at Old Trafford a complete unknown on these shores, but finished it with 17 Premiership goals and as United's top scorer for the season

Honours
Premiership [1997]

Transfers
FK Clausengen to Molde FK
Molde FK to Man Utd [£1.5m]

Position/Role
Fooling defenders into letting him score by pretending he's just nipping down the sweetshop

Word most often used to describe him
Youthful

Word never used to describe him
Useful

> "When I head towards goal I know exactly what to do."
>
> *Ole Gunnar Solskjaer*

le Gunnar Solskjaer likes to keep things simple – on and off the pitch. When he's playing for Manchester United he simply likes to get the ball and stick it in the back of the net. And when he's not playing football, he admits to preferring a simple night in at home than a night out on the tiles.

"I love playing for United. I love the atmosphere," he says. "But I am an ordinary guy." However, since arriving at Old Trafford from Norwegian side Molde for a bargain basement £1.5 million in the summer of 1996, this is one guy whose form has been anything but 'ordinary'. His performances have been so impressive that he's sure to have earned himself a pay rise over the summer, and yet when he went out to treat himself to a BMW recently he managed to find himself a secondhand bargain.

Life, though, isn't as simple for Solskjaer as it might be. Amazingly, the 24-year-old is allergic to grass. If he doesn't take the right medication he'll end up having a sneezing fit. "I try not to make a big deal out of it," he says. "But I know it's crazy for someone who spends half his life running around on grass." Dust is also a problem, and when he and his girlfriend, Silge, moved into Andrei Kanchelskis's old house in Cheshire they had to have all the carpets removed and the whole place swept clean.

If he keeps playing like he has been, however, Alex Ferguson won't be worried. Ferguson initially saw Solskjaer as a long term buy – one for the future – but as soon as he was given a chance, Ole Gunnar realised (if you'll excuse the pun) it was not to be sniffed at. Scoring after six minutes of his first appearance as substitute, Solskjaer hasn't looked back.

"I find it easy to score goals," Solskjaer explains. "When I head towards goal I know exactly what to do. Being an unknown before I came here has helped me. If you come to a club with a huge reputation, it can be difficult, but when I got the chance the fans didn't expect a lot from me. I'm just glad of every minute I play."

He's not the only one.

Vital Statistics

Age 26

Date of Birth 3.9.70

Place of Birth Watford

League games & goals
Crystal Palace 152 [15]
Aston Villa 58 [2]

Transfers
Crystal Palce to Aston Villa [£2.5m]

Gareth Southgate's 1996/97 season
Lost his England place but continued to perform consistently for Villa, although injury problems hampered his season

Position/Role
Classy defending and intelligent use of the ball once he's won it... just don't let him take the penalties!

Word most often used to describe him
Honest

Word[s] never used to describe him
Penalty expert

"I'll probably practice penalties a bit more..."

Gareth Southgate

Gareth SOUTHGATE

If you work it out, Gareth Southgate has probably kicked the ball about fifty thousand times in his professional career. Which makes it all the more heart-breaking that he will probably always be remembered for just one of them – that weak penalty in the Euro '96 semi-final that made German goalkeeper, Kopke, look like a dad giving his toddler son shooting practice in the park!

Southgate, helped by a little counselling from Pearce and Waddle and a wad of cash for a pizza commercial with the same two, has recovered remarkably well from the trauma, despite being reminded of it every day.

"It crops up on TV when you least expect it to," says the Aston Villa central defender/sweeper. "I was watching a documentary about hooliganism and suddenly there I was hitting the ball at Kopke. They cut into the reaction at the bar. That cheered me up no end seeing everyone crying, groaning and holding their heads."

Since then, Southgate has taken a lot of stick from opposing fans. In his first away game after the tournament, Villa were awarded a penalty against Derby County. "The whole of the ground was chanting my name before Tommy Johnson stepped up to take it," he remembers wryly.

The best way to silence the critics is to outplay the teams they support and Southgate has relished the free-man-in-the-defence role that Brian Little gives him at Villa. "I enjoy being able to create from defence. It's certainly the way forward and most of our Premiership teams are doing it now."

The reality is that Southgate, who has been tipped by many as a future England captain, often gets the opportunity to score in his free role at the back. But would he ever take another penalty? "I'll probably practice penalties a bit more than I did and, faced with a similar situation, yes, I would have to take one again."

Can you imagine it? France '98, England face West Germany in the semi final. The game is still 1-1 after 120 minutes to play, it's 5-5 in the penalty shoot-out.

Reebok
AST
COMPUTER

Vital Statistics

Age 29

Date of Birth 6.9.67

Place of Birth
Metkovic [Croatia]

League Games & Goals
Dinamo Vinklovic [former Yugoslavia]
Cadiz [Spain]
Hadjuk Split [Croatia]
Derby County 60 [2]

Honours
Croation League & Cup [1995]

Did you know?
Stimac could have signed for Cologne in Germany or Vicenza in Italy but chose Derby County [then in the first division] instead

Word most often used to describe him
Stylish

Word never used to describe him
Clogger

"With these fine supporters behind me I am happy."

Igor Stimac

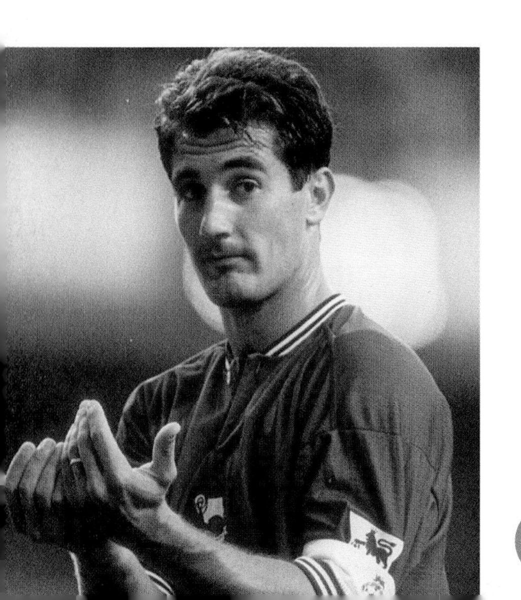

When Derby County move into their new Pride Park stadium this season, it surely won't be long before the brand spanking new rafters are reverberating to the chant of "Igor, Igor" whenever Derby's Croatian international sweeper/central defender, Igor Stimac, does something good, which is rather often. They love Stimac at Derby and they've every right to. The 29-year-old was the missing piece which finally completed the promotion jigsaw out of Division One and into the Premiership two seasons ago, and he has been outstanding ever since.

Stimac plays the vital man role in Derby's five-strong defence, and it is his favourite position - he is sometimes forced into a full back berth for the Croatian national team. He is a defender in the style of Alan Hansen or Franco Baresi, an astute reader of the game who can play with the ball a bit. And at 6ft 4ins, he's no slouch in the air either.

Stimac, then, was a bit of a snip at £1.7 million (if such a thing exists), although hardly any Derby fans had ever heard of him when he arrived at the club, with hardly a word of English in his head, back in November 1995.

Stimac was rather well-known in his home country, however, as skipper of the Hajduk Split team which had just won the Croatian League and Cup double and had got to the quarter finals of the European Cup, as well as an automatic choice for the national team.

Derby's gain was Cologne and Vicenza's loss. Both were after him, but Stimac liked the feel of the surroundings in the Midlands most. "I can understand people's surprise that I should have signed for Derby," he said after the move. "The captain of our national side, Boban, plays for Milan, others play for Barcelona and Lazio. But it is important to feel comfortable where you are living, especially when you have a family."

And the First Division looks a long way away now, as Derby prepare for their second season in the Premiership. Stimac is confident about the future. "As captain of Hajduk I achieved a lot of success and I don't see why that should change at Derby," he says.

Igor STIMAC

PUMA

JVC

Vital Statistics

Age 21

Date of Birth 23.6.76

Place of Birth
Dakar, Senegal

League Games & Goals
Tours
Cannes
AC Milan 2 [0]
Arsenal 35 [2]

International record
Viera has played for France at all levels, making his full debut in 1997 against Holland. At the time of writing he had made two full appearances

Transfers
Tours to Cannes
Cannes to AC Milan [£3.5m]
AC Milan to Arsenal [£1.5m]

Position/Role
Bringing to life the phrase 'an old head on young shoulders'

Word most often used to describe him
What?

Word never used to describe him
Veteran

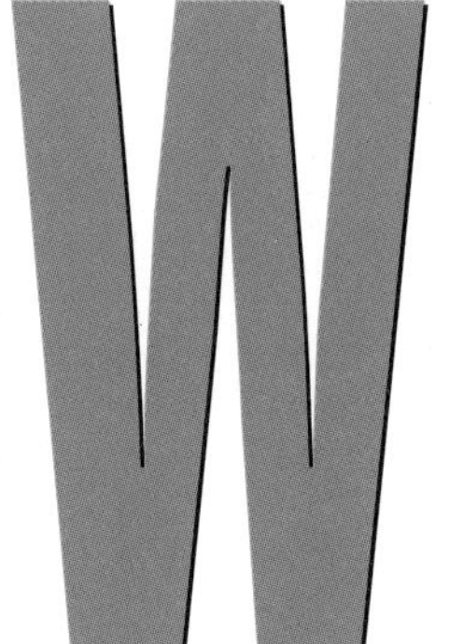

hen the Highbury faithful heard the news about their new signing from AC Milan last season, they asked, "Patrick who?". It didn't take long though before the name 'Viera' was booming out from the stands at Highbury.

Viera – Arsene Wenger's first signing (Bruce Rioch was still manager when he began secret negotiations with the player), has been what you'd call an instant hit in the Gunners' midfield, mixing battling graft with continental craft. "He reads the game well. He has quick feet and he's a good passer," glows his compatriot Wenger. "The other players accepted him straight away because they could see he was a team player."

Just like their fans, though, the other Arsenal players weren't sure about the name. When he first arrived they just called him 'what?', mimicking his answer to every question they asked him.

It was all taken in good spirit though, and it is the spirit shown by his Highbury team-mates that the young Frenchman is still trying to come to terms with. "I have never known a desire and will to win like it," he explains. "It is the difference between England and other countries."

Still only 21, Viera (who was born in Dakar, Senegal but moved to Paris at the age of seven), first caught Wenger's eye playing in France for Tours and then Cannes, whom he captained at the age of 19. It wasn't long before AC Milan snapped him up for £3.5 million and that seemed to be that, but six months later he was for sale again.

"I could not believe my luck," says Wenger. "Milan do not usually sign a 20-year-old player and let him go just months later. I told Arsene to move quickly and not to wait. I've seen Milan officials since and they admit they made a mistake."

And the Arsenal manager's first-ever signing for the club could just turn out to be his most significant. "He can become a future Arsenal captain," adds Wenger. "He has good technique and he's a winner. Outside the field he gives the impression of being soft and casual. But on the field he is a fighter. Nothing frightens him."

> "...on the field he's a fighter. Nothing frightens him."
>
> *Arsene Wenger*

Vital Statistics

Age 25

Date of Birth 31.10.71

Place of Birth Watford

League Games & Goals
Oxford 2
Spurs 163

Ian Walker's 1996/97 season
Despite injury problems and a drop in form, Walker played in all but one of Tottenham's games and, of course, that infamous February night for England against Italy

Position/Role
Usually safe hands, silly haircut

Did you know?
Ian Walker posed nude for a woman's magazine in the White Hart Lane changing rooms

Word most often used to describe him
Cool

Word never used to describe him
Stress

It's been said of too many promising young goalkeepers, but we're going to say it again - Ian Walker looks like he could well be the England keeper for years to come, when he finally displaces David Seaman from the number one spot. Despite a disappointing season in 1995/96 - which included letting Gianfranco Zola's goal for Italy in at the near post at Wembley – he still looks the best of the young crop of goalkeepers in England's ranks.

One man who, not surprisingly, agrees is another former professional goalkeeper – and more famously manager of Norwich City – Mike Walker, his dad. "Ian's positional play and his handling are very strong," says the former Everton boss, now back at Carrow Road. "They have been from an early age – and I'm talking six or seven. But his main strength is his temperament, which is very good.

"You look at all the best goalkeepers of the past like Banks, like Jennings, like Shilton, and they've all had very good composure. Ian's the same. Maybe it's rubbed off from me a bit, I never get too excited."

Walker Jr. certainly has had many experienced keepers in close proximity to coach him. "He's been very lucky," says Walker Sr. "When he arrived at Tottenham Ray Clemence was there, and now Pat Jennings is at White Hart Lane as goalkeeping coach."

The 6 ft 1 inch keeper isn't far off being a kid now; he's still just 25, though you wouldn't think it when you look back on a career that started in 1990. This is only the second full season he's had at Tottenham, though, having finally wrested the number one jersey from Eric Thorsvedt.

"His next step is to get into the England team and stay there," says his father. "He's always been adamant from an early age that that's what he wants to do. And he's a determined man. It's the kind of calm determination, which is often confused for a lack of passion. Nothing could be further from the truth."

As a parting shot, we asked Dad Walker if his son has any weaknesses. To my surprise he gives me an answer. "Maybe he could stand up a little more," he says, semi-cryptically. Premiership strikers take note – hear it from a man who knows.

> "Ian has a kind of calm determination."
>
> *Ian's Dad, Mike Walker*

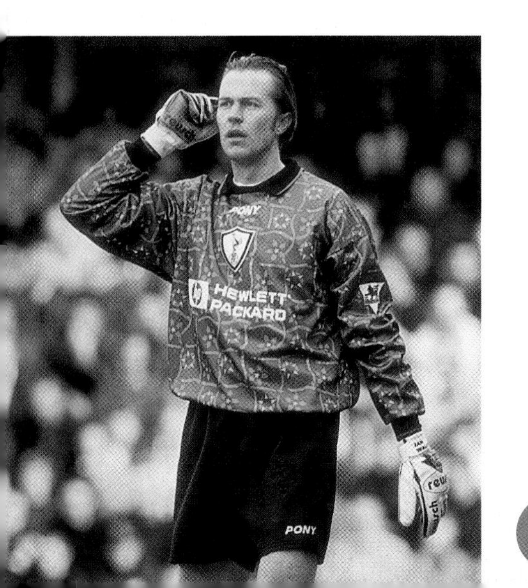

UMBRO
CFC
Coors

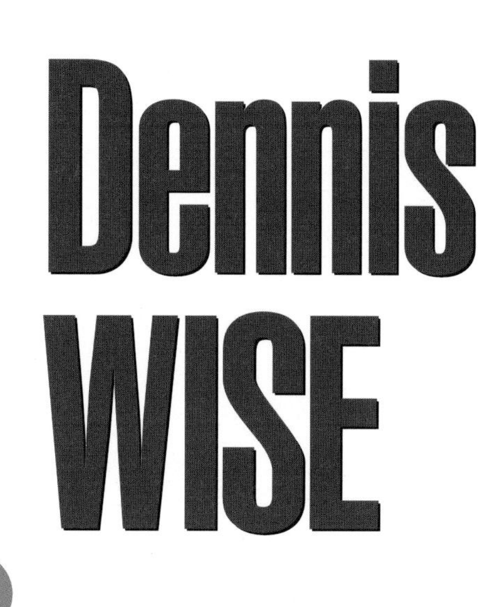

Vital Statistics

Age 30

Date of Birth 15.12.66

Place of Birth London

Nickname The Rat

League Games & Goals
Wimbledon 135 [27]
Chelsea 187 [40]

Dennis Wise's 1996/97 season
Kept his place in Ruud Gullit's foreign legion, playing in 27 of the club's league games and scoring eight goals

Honours
FA Cup [Wimbledon] [1988]

Transfers
Wimbledon to Chelsea [£1.6m]

Position/Role
Letting his feet do the talking, thank goodness

Word most often used to describe him
Squeaky

Word never used to describe him
Lofty

A crafty little long-haired genius from Italy might have been hogging the limelight at Chelsea this season – but a short, pasty skinhead by the name of Dennis Wise has been revelling in Gianfranco Zola's shadow. For while the footballing world drools over Zola's masterful ability, he of the cheeky grin and high-pitched voice has continued with good, consistent form.

Now skipper of a Chelsea side looking ahead to a bright future and playing the best football of his life, it's all a long way from being rejected by Southampton for being 'too small'. It was then that he was picked up on a 'free' by Wimbledon where he became the arch-provider for arch-finisher, John Fashanu.

In Wimbledon's 1987/88 FA Cup-winning year, statistics showed he was the provider or scorer of no fewer than 75 per cent of the Dons' goals.

A £1.6 million move to Chelsea followed before the 1990/91 season and, despite the occasional disciplinary blemish (both on and off the pitch), he's just about been Chelsea's most consistent player (albeit over five years of miserable inconsistency), ever since.

Wise combines tough-tackling and hard-running with supreme natural skill and ball control, the ability to pick out passes which even his manager, Ruud Gullit, would be proud of, and a dead ball expertise for which he has few rivals in the Premiership.

A cheeky chappy if ever there was one, Wise did have one run-in with the new gaffer when Gullit took over the helm at Stamford Bridge. He was cooly informed that it would not be helpful to his first team prospects if he continued to refer to the manager as 'big nose'. Since then, he's knuckled down alongside Roberto Di Matteo in the Anglo-Italian Chelsea midfield, growing in stature just like the stadium (and the club) around him.

Last season's success in the FA Cup may have been inspired by Zola and masterminded by Gullit, but if Chelsea ever do start to really tick in the Premiership you can bet your last tube of hair gel that little Dennis Wise will be right at the heart of it.

> “Perfect happiness is a few beers after a Chelsea victory.”
>
> *Dennis Wise*

Vital Statistics

Age 33

Date of Birth 3.11.63

Place of Birth Woolwich

League Games & Goals
Crystal Palace 225 [90]
Arsenal 192 [118]

Honours
FA Cup [1993]
League Cup [1993]

Transfers
Greenwich Boro to Palace [free]
Palace to Arsenal [£2.5m]

Position/Role
Running around like a man possessed, scoring goals and getting booked

Did you know?
Ian Wright has a tattoo of a Harley Davidson motorbike on his right thigh!

Word most often used to describe him
Clinical

Word never used to describe him
Past-it

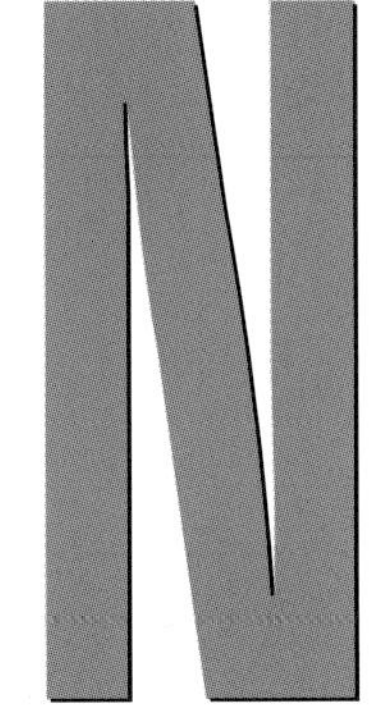

New York may be so good they named it twice, but Ian Wright is so good he goes one better. 'Ian Wright, Wright, Wright', is a one-man scoring machine. With his heart on his sleeve, his emotions always on the boil, and the ball invariably nestling in the Highbury net, his name has become synonymous with scoring goals for Arsenal. Wright is just a handful of strikes away from breaking Cliff Bastin's all-time scoring record for the Gunners of 178 goals. After he scored his 100th Arsenal goal, the club's vice-chairman gave him a piece of paper. It said, 'Cliff Bastin 178, John Radford 149, Ian Wright 100'. "That's my goal," said Wright pointing immediately at Bastin's record.

When Arsene Wenger arrived at the club, many felt that the older players were likely to be on the receiving end of a major clear-out by the Frenchman. Wright would have missed his chance. But the new manager couldn't have been more impressed by the attitude of the striker who claims people's view of him as a 'big-time Charlie' is 'all wrong.'

At 33, he might be getting on a bit, but the fire still rages ferociously inside his belly and let's face it, if you were a defender you wouldn't want to face him.

Signed from Palace in 1991, Wright has done more than anyone since then to explode the 'boring, boring Arsenal' myth. And although there's so much more to his game than sticking the ball in the onion bag, it's his thirst for goal-scoring glory that drives him on.

"All I see at the end of the season is the golden boot," he says. "That's what I go for, and I know if I score enough goals at the end of the season I'll get that. I'd rather score two goals from tap-ins than one that's a bit special, but I must say I do love scoring spectacular goals. To score a goal that ordinary people won't be able to score is what you have to aim for."

And there's only one place he wants to do it. "I love this club," he says. "I want my legacy to be that every time I played I didn't cheat the club. I gave 110 per cent and some good goals. They've treated me fantastically and I just want them to think of me with a smile." Not much to ask, really, from your record goalscorer of all time.

> "I must say I do love scoring spectacular goals."
>
> *Ian Wright*

JVC

Coors

Gianfranco ZOLA

Vital Statistics

Age 31

Date of Birth 5.7.66

Place of Birth Sardinia, Italy

League Games & Goals
Nicorese [Italy] 31 [10]
Torres [Italy] 88 [21]
Napoli 105 [32]
Parma 102 [49]
Chelsea 23 [8]

International record
Zola made his debut for Italy in 1991 and at the time of writing had scored 10 goals in 31 games for his country [including one rather important one at Wembley]

Honours
Italian Championship [Napoli] [1990]
UEFA Cup [Parma] [1995]
FA Cup [1997]
Football Writers' Player of the Year [1997]

Position/Role
Running around and making Chelsea fans think they've died and gone to heaven

Word most often used to describe him
Indescribable

Word[s] never used to describe him
Big man

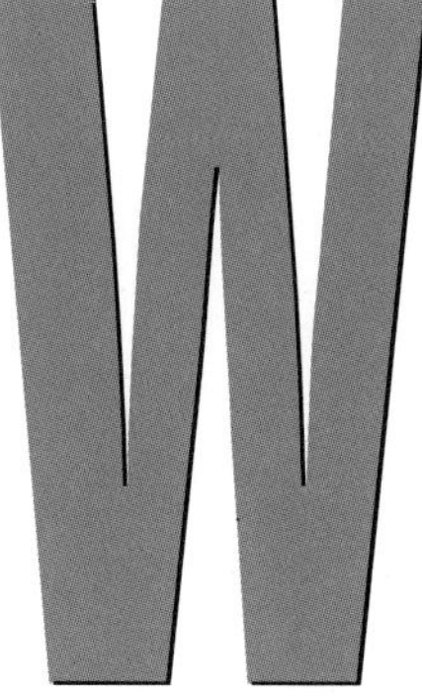

When 5ft 5in Gianfranco Zola joined Chelsea, the club had an immediate problem with their £4.5 million man. Their XL shirts were too big for him. Chelsea soon made some smaller ones though, and the Sardinian-born attacker has since fitted perfectly into the English game.

So perfectly, in fact, that the Italian international star is very possibly the most gifted player in the Premiership. His passing is sublime – whether it's a short five-yarder that puts out a defender or a pinpoint forty-yarder that bypasses the whole of the opposition midfield – and his free-kicks... well, his free-kicks are something else.

It won't come as much of a surprise to learn that his mentor, as a youngster at Napoli, was none other than Diego Maradona. "He would stay after training teaching me how to curl the ball at free kicks," remembers the 30-year-old. "The first time I replaced him in the team we were playing Ascoli and I was having a nightmare. Everything was going wrong for me – I could hardly kick a ball straight. Then right at the end we got a free kick and I pleaded with my teammates to let me take it. I thought it was going to hit the corner flag but then it suddenly curled and went in. I just turned round and there were 60,000 people going mad."

Plenty more free kicks have 'suddenly curled' since then. Zola is reckoned to have the incredible strike rate of more than one in three from around the box and is reckoned to be the best free kick expert ever to have played in Italy, with a better average than Zico, Platini, and even his mentor, Maradona.

Zola's first taste of English football was in 1990 when he played for a scratch team against the England World Cup team – he finished the wrong side of a 10-2 drubbing. Next up was Parma's 1995 European Cup Winners' Cup final defeat against Arsenal. Since his Chelsea debut against Blackburn last year, however, he's acclimatised superbly to the English game - a fact which was cruelly underlined when he broke millions of English hearts by flicking the ball past Ian Walker in the vital World Cup qualifier at Wembley last February.

> "Are you sure the people who voted for me weren't drunk?"
>
> *1997 Footballer of the Year, G Zola*

Predictions for the

Trying to predict how the league table will look at the end of the season is about as easy as trying to get Kenny Dalglish to smile or Alex Ferguson to admit the referee was spot-on! We're not afraid to make fools of ourselves, though, and we're confident that the Premiership table will turn out something like this...

Predicted final table 1997/98

1 Arsenal	6 Aston Villa	11 Tottenham	16 Crystal Palace
2 Manchester Utd	7 Leeds Utd	12 Wimbledon	17 Derby County
3 Newcastle Utd	8 Sheffield Wed	13 Bolton	18 Southampton
4 Liverpool	9 Blackburn R	14 Coventry	19 West Ham
5 Chelsea	10 Everton	15 Leicester City	20 Barnsley

Arsenal

Prediction 1st

It's hard to see anyone wrenching the title from the grasp of Manchester United, but if anyone can, Arsene's Arsenal can. Not since 1991 has the championship trophy nestled in a London club's trophy cabinet, but wily Frenchman Wenger nearly managed it last season with an ageing side plus Patrick Viera, and this time he'll have added even further in the French Foreign Legion department. Wenger seems to be snapping up all the best young French stars and bringing them to Highbury, and with the likes of Wright, Merson and Adams maintaining the English hunger and steel (not to mention a fair dose of talent), the Gunners could be one hell of a side this season.

Manchester United

Prediction 2nd

OK, so they'll probably win it again but we had to go for something different didn't we? The only thing which could blow our theory is that winning the title has become something of a habit. In the last six years, United have won it four times and finished second (by a whisker) twice. But maybe, just maybe, this is one of those rare runners-up years. With United bound to concentrate even harder on the Champions League and winning the European Cup (Ferguson's obsession), this could be the year when someone else nicks in and grabs the glory. It is hard to spot a weakness in the United set-up, but there's no doubt that the opposition is getting stronger.

Newcastle United

Prediction 3rd

It has to be all-change time at St James' Park, with Dalglish rebuilding the side which Keegan took so close, but which ultimately proved not good enough. Every team needs solid foundations, but Newcastle have been trying to build their dream of winning their first title in 70 years, on a bed of quicksand. A stunning array of the world's finest striking talent is only half as effective as it should be when you've got a defence with more holes than a Swiss cheese! Dalglish knows he must tackle the problem, and tackle it he surely will. Whether he'll have time to get the Toon Army firing on all cylinders for a title push, though, remains to be seen.

PREMIER LEAGUE

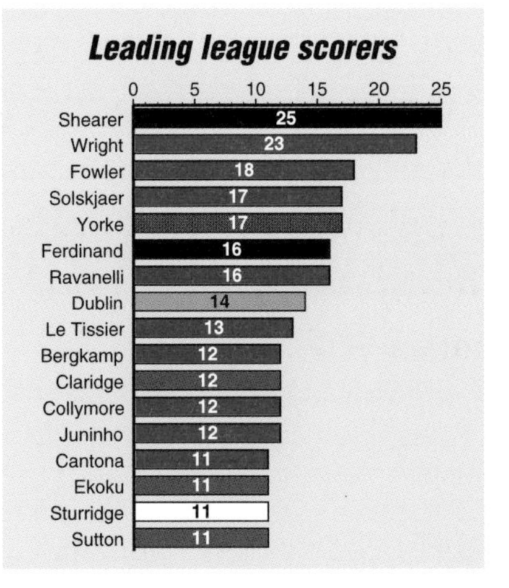

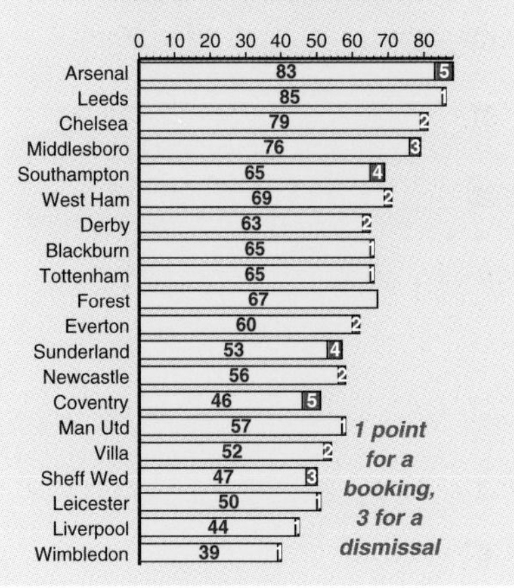

Leading scorers

0 4 8 12 16 20 24 28

Fowler 18 5 1 7
Ravanelli 16 9 6
Wright 23 5 2
Shearer 25 1 1 1
Ferdinand 16 1 4
Yorke 17 1 2
Solskjaer 17 1
Le Tissier 13 3
Collymore 12 2 2
Claridge 12 2 1
Juninho 12 1 2
Dublin 14
Bergkamp 12 1 1
Cantona 11 3
Sturridge 11 1 2
Ostenstad 10 3 1
Hughes 8 1 5

League goals in club colour, Coca Cola in Purple, FA in Orange. European in Brown

Liverpool

Prediction 4th

Last year was surely Liverpool's chance. They were in the driving seat but then, literally in the case of David James, threw it away. Let's face it, the Liverpool team are too pretty to win the title. You wouldn't catch Gary and Phil Neville cavorting around nightclubs with supermodels, and unless Roy Evans bolsters his team with a few ugly blokes then another season of failure looms at Anfield.

Aston Villa

Prediction 6th

As money talks louder and louder in football, Manchester United, Arsenal, Liverpool and Newcastle have moved into a mini-league of their own. Aston Villa, however, are the club most consistently knocking on the door and trying to get in. You just sense, though, that it would take a couple of really sensational signings (like Stan Collymore?), to get them past that big, meaty bouncer on the door.

Leeds United

Prediction 7th

Well, George Graham certainly has a track record of winning championships. Unfortunately, he also has a track record of producing extremely dull, defensive football teams. By the end of last season, he'd achieved the second of those objectives at Elland Road, the question is can he achieve the first? Probably not this season, and how long will the Leeds fans put up with a dull team that isn't winning the league?

Chelsea

Prediction 5th

The alarm clock has gone off and the kettle is boiling... the sleeping giant is rousing. Trouble is, we keep saying that about Chelsea and the Blues keep pressing the snooze button and snatching another season's kip. OK, so they won the FA Cup and, yes, they've got some quality players and an impressive stadium but, frankly, so has everyone else and a place in Europe is all they can hope for.

Sheffield Wednesday

Prediction 8th
If Sheffield Wednesday's middle of last season had been anything like the beginning and the end, then David Pleat's side might have won the title. Without exactly grabbing the headlines, Wednesday were always neat, efficient and occasionally spectacular. There seems to be money in the bank to strengthen the side at Hillsborough, although last season will be a tough act to follow.

Blackburn R

Prediction 9th
A few years ago, no one in England had heard of Roy Hodgson. A little known English coach, he turned up in charge of Switzerland then was taken on by Inter Milan and people had to take notice. Ewood Park expects great things, but Rovers' position of power has been diminished now that everyone else has as much money as them. He hasn't got an easy job!

Everton

Prediction 10th
From outside, Goodison Park events at Everton in recent years have been farcical, but from within the club the whole thing has gone beyond a joke. Millions have been spent, yet recent seasons have ended in a relegation dogfight. There is money to spend and incredible support to tap into, but it will take more than one season to stop everyone else from laughing.

Tottenham Hotspur

Prediction 11th
Remember when Spurs were a big club? Remember when, even if they lost, they had star names and always played attractive football? Well those were the days before Alan Sugar arrived. OK, he saved the club, but his 'sound business sense' has condemned it to years of dull underachievement. Going to White Hart Lane used to be a thrill, these days it's a drag.

Wimbledon

Prediction 12th
Poor old Wimbledon! At one stage still in the running for all competitions, they ended up with nothing - not even a trip to some desolate eastern European country in the UEFA Cup. If anyone can lift his troops and rally the Dons again, it is Joe Kinnear, but you get the feeling that last season was the best chance of a trophy they were going to get in years.

Bolton Wanderers

Prediction 13th
First they were up, then they were down, now they are up again with a stronger, more experienced, squad and a brand new stadium. Colin Todd's side were just getting used to the top flight when they were relegated two seasons ago, and that cruel initiation to the Premiership will ensure they don't make the same mistake twice.

Coventry City

Prediction 14th
There seems to be some sort of opposite gravitational pull ensuring Premiership survival for Coventry. Come the latter stages of every season, the entire population of the city is forced to walk around with their hearts in their mouths. They always know deep down, however, that the force is with them.

Highest Attendances

Club	Attendance
Man Utd	55,314
Liverpool	40,892
Everton	40,177
Leeds	39,981
Aston Villa	39,339
Sheff Wed	38,943
Arsenal	38,264
Newcastle	36,582
Tottenham	33,040
Blackburn	30,476
Middlesbrough	30,215
Nott'm Forest	29,181
Chelsea	28,418
Wimbledon	25,786
West Ham	25,064
Coventry	23,085
Sunderland	22,512
Leicester	21,134
Derby	18,287
Southampton	15,253

Lowest Attendances

Club	Attendance
Man Utd	54,178
Newcastle	36,143
Liverpool	36,126
Arsenal	33,461
Everton	30,368
Middlesbrough	29,485
Aston Villa	26,726
Leeds	25,860
Chelsea	24,027
Tottenham	22,943
Blackburn	19,214
West Ham	19,105
Sunderland	18,642
Leicester	17,562
Nott'm Forest	17,525
Derby	17,022
Sheff Wed	16,390
Coventry	15,273
Southampton	14,418
Wimbledon	7,979

Club Bad Boys

		Red	Yellow
Arsenal	Wright	1	10
Villa	Staunton	1	5
	Townsend		8
Blackburn	McKinlay		12
Chelsea	Leboeuf	1	7
Coventry City	Whelan	1	9
Derby County	Powell D	1	7
	Stimac		10
Everton	Unsworth	1	6
	Ferguson	1	6
Leeds Utd	Palmer	1	11
Leicester	Lennon		8
	Heskey		8
Liverpool	Fowler	1	4
Man Utd	Keane	1	6
Middlesbrough	Mustoe		10
Newcastle	Batty	1	10
Nottm Forest	Pearce		8
Sheff Wed	Atherton		7
	Pembridge		7
Southampton	van Gobbel	1	10
Sunderland	Ord	2	3
Tottenham	Edinburgh		11
West Ham	Bilic		11
Wimbledon	Jones	1	5

Leicester City

Prediction 15th

Well, Leicester proved everyone wrong last season didn't they? Martin O'Neill proved that not only could he motivate Barnet to beat Brazil, he could also assemble a highly skilful and committed bunch of players. Premiership survival and a Coca Cola Cup win were monster achievements, this time O'Neill will be going for 'the double'!

Crystal Palace

Prediction 16th

So Palace are up again, just as ex-manager Dave Bassett drops back down with Forest. The Eagles have some highly-talented young players at Selhurst Park and, if chairman Ron Noades sticks his hand in his pocket to buy a couple of more experienced players, they should survive.

Derby County

Prediction 17th

This will be a tough old season for the Rams, but survival last time around will have them well prepared for the battle ahead. The unfamiliar surroundings of their brand spanking new stadium in Pride Park may not be an advantage as teams used to fear a trip to the Baseball Ground, but with Sturridge, Asanovic and Stimac they have the quality to stay up... just!

Southampton

Prediction 18th

Well, it had to happen sometime didn't it? The Saints have been flirting with relegation for years, relying on Matt Le Tissier to save them every time. This time it could well be 'a season too far' for the south coasters, victims partly because of their 15,000 capacity ground which leaves them with smaller average crowds than Wimbledon.

West Ham

Prediction 19th

Will the hammer finally come down on the Hammers? Last season turned into a disaster with foreign signing after foreign signing turning out to be a case of 'what a waste of money'. With John Hartson and Julian Dicks in the side, you can bet your last jellied eel they'll go down fighting, but this could be the season the bubble finally bursts.

Barnsley

Prediction 20th

Danny Wilson did a tremendous job getting Barnsley into the top flight for the first time in their history, but staying there is going to be the tough bit. Wilson's team played their way out of Division One in a style which will certainly grace the Premiership, but they'll have to step it up a gear or two to prove us wrong about the drop.

1997/98 Premier

Top 'Goalscorers'

Alan Shearer	25
Ian Wright	21
Robbie Fowler	18
Dwight Yorke	17
Ole Solskjaer	17
Fabrizio Ravanelli	16
Dion Dublin	14
Matt Le Tissier	13
Stan Collymore	12

Top 'leaky' defences

Middlesbrough (conceded)	60
Nott'm Forest	59
Derby County	58
Everton	57
Southampton	56
Chelsea	55
Coventry City	54
Sunderland	53
Sheff Wed	51
Tottenham	51

Top 10 'meanest' defences

Arsenal (conceded)	32
Liverpool	37
Leeds Utd	38
Newcastle Utd	40
Blackburn R	43
Aston Villa	44
Man Utd	44
Wimbledon	46
West Ham	48
Leicester	50

11 teams who earned the most 0-0 draws

Leeds Utd	9
West Ham	6
Blackburn R	6
Coventry City	6
Aston Villa	5
Sheff Wed	5
Arsenal	4
Derby County	4
Middlesbrough	4
Nott'm Forest	4
Sunderland	4

Top 'highest' scoring teams

Man Utd	76
Newcastle Utd	73
Arsenal	62
Liverpool	62
Chelsea	58
Sheff Wed	50
Middlesbrough	51
Wimbledon	49
Aston Villa	47
Leicester	46

Top 'lowest' scoring teams

Everton	44
Tottenham	44
Blackburn R	42
Southampton	40
West Ham	39
Coventry City	38
Sunderland	35
Nott'm Forest	31
Leeds Utd	28

Top 'best' supported teams

1. Man Utd
2. Liverpool
3. Arsenal
4. Newcastle Utd
5. Everton
6. Aston Villa
7. Leeds Utd
8. Middlesbrough
9. Tottenham
10. Chelsea

League Stats

Top 'worst' supported teams

1. Wimbledon
2. Southampton
3. Derby County
4. Coventry City
5. Leicester
6. Sunderland
7. West Ham
8. Blackburn R
9. Sheff Wed
10. Nott'm Forest

Top 'Games' with the most goals

Southampton	6	v	Man Utd	3	*9 goals*
Chelsea	6	v	Southampton	2	*8 goals*
Everton	7	v	Southampton	1	*8 goals*
Newcastle Utd	7	v	Tottenham	1	*8 goals*
Liverpool	4	v	Newcastle Utd	3	*7 goals*
Middlesbrough	6	v	Derby County	1	*7 goals*
Newcastle Utd	4	v	Aston Villa	3	*7 goals*
Newcastle Utd	4	v	Leicester	3	*7 goals*
West Ham	4	v	Tottenham	3	*7 goals*
Chelsea	2	v	Wimbledon	4	*6 goals*

11 teams with the most players sent off

Arsenal	5
Coventry City	5
Sunderland	5
Southampton	4
Middlesbrough	3
Sheff Wed	3
Aston Villa	2
Derby County	2
Everton	2
Newcastle Utd	2
West Ham	2

10 teams with the most away wins

Arsenal	9
Liverpool	9
Man Utd	9
Chelsea	7
Aston Villa	6
Newcastle Utd	6
Sheff Wed	6
Wimbledon	6
Leicester	5
Tottenham	5

10 clubs with the most home wins

Newcastle Utd	13
Man Utd	12
Aston Villa	11
Arsenal	10
Liverpool	10
Chelsea	9
Wimbledon	9
Blackburn R	8
Derby County	8
Middlesbrough	8

10 teams with the most bookings

Arsenal	84
Leeds Utd	81
Middlesbrough	78
Chelsea	74
Southampton	67
Blackburn R	65
Nott'm Forest	64
Tottenham	64
West Ham	64
Derby County	62